Explorers of the NEW WORLD

Discover the Golden Age of Exploration

Carla Mooney
Illustrated by Tom Casteel

Titles in the *Build It Yourself* Series

green press
INITIATIVE

Nomad Press is committed to preserving ancient forests and natural resources. We elected to print *Explorers of the New World* on 4,007 lbs. of Williamsburg Recycled 30% offset.

Nomad Press made this paper choice because our printer, Sheridan Books, is a member of Green Press Initiative, a nonprofit program dedicated to supporting authors, publishers, and suppliers in their efforts to reduce their use of fiber obtained from endangered forests. For more information, visit **www.greenpressinitiative.org**

Nomad Press
A division of Nomad Communications
10 9 8 7 6 5 4 3 2 1

This book was manufactured by Sheridan Books,
Ann Arbor, MI USA.
July 2011, Job #327482
ISBN: 978-1-936313-44-0

Illustrations by Tom Casteel
Educational Consultant, Marla Conn

Questions regarding the ordering of this book should be addressed to
Independent Publishers Group
814 N. Franklin St.
Chicago, IL 60610
www.ipgbook.com

Nomad Press
2456 Christian St.
White River Junction, VT 05001
www.nomadpress.net

CONTENTS

Timeline: The Golden Age of Exploration

1002
Leif Erikson discovers North America.

1271-95
Marco Polo journeys to China, establishing the overland trade route.

1405
Admiral Zheng begins his voyages for China. His fleet rules the South Pacific and Indian Ocean until 1433.

1419
Prince Henry the Navigator establishes a naval observatory for teaching navigation, astronomy, and cartography.

1420
Portuguese navigators discover and settle the Madeiras, a group of islands 400 miles off the northwest coast of Africa.

1434
One of Prince Henry's captains, Gil Eanes, rounds Cape Bojador on the northwest coast of Africa.

1441
Portuguese begin Atlantic slave trade.

1453
Turks overrun Constantinople, shutting off the overland trade route to China. Prices for spices and silks soar.

1488
Bartolomeau Dias lands at the Cape of Good Hope on the southern tip of Africa.

1492
Christopher Columbus sets sail on his first voyage and claims the Caribbean for Spain.

1493
Columbus returns from his first voyage and sets sail on his second voyage to the New World in September.

1494
The Treaty of Tordesillas divides the world between Spain and Portugal.

1497
John Cabot sets out from England to find a shorter western route across the Atlantic Ocean to the Indies. He discovers Newfoundland and the North American continent. Vasco da Gama sails from Portugal and rounds the Cape of Good Hope.

1498
Da Gama reaches India and establishes an important trade route for Portugal. Columbus sets out on his third voyage to the New World. Cabot sails on his second voyage to North America.

1500
Pedro Álvares Cabral gets lost in a storm and lands in Brazil, on the east coast of South America.

Timeline: The Golden Age of Exploration

1502
Columbus sails on his fourth and final voyage to the New World.

1506
Columbus dies in Spain.

1513
Ponce de León lands in Florida.

1519
Ferdinand Magellan begins his journey to circumnavigate the world. Hernán Cortés leads an expedition to find the rich Aztec kingdom in Mexico.

1521
Magellan reaches the Philippines. Combining this trip west with an earlier trip east to the Philippines, he becomes the first man to sail around the world. On April 27, Magellan is killed by natives in the Philippines.

1522
On September 6, Magellan's crew returns on one ship, with just 18 having completed the voyage to circumnavigate the world.

1526-27
Francisco Pizarro sails on his second voyage down the coast of South America.

1532
Pizarro captures the Inca ruler, Atahualpa.

1535
Jacques Cartier sails up the St. Lawrence River and claims the land for France.

1539
Hernando de Soto begins exploration of the southeastern United States, killing and enslaving the local people.

1540
Francisco de Coronado travels in the southwestern United States, looking for the fabled Seven Cities of Cibola.

1541
Cartier founds France's first colony in the New World and names it Charlesbourg-Royal. Pizarro is murdered in Peru. De Soto becomes the first European to see the Mississippi River.

1577-80
Sir Francis Drake sails from England and circumnavigates the globe.

1604
Samuel de Champlain sails from France to start a settlement in Acadia, Maine.

1607
Henry Hudson attempts to find the Northwest Passage by sailing across the North Pole.

1608
Champlain founds present-day Quebec City, in Canada.

1609
Hudson explores present-day New York and the Hudson River, claiming both for the Dutch.

1610
Hudson's crew mutinies and sets him adrift in a rowboat. Hudson is never seen again.

Introduction

Exploring in the Age of Discovery

Since the dawn of time, humans have been exploring the unknown. Their reasons have been many—to find new sources of food, spread a religion, or trade goods. The excitement of discovery inspired the explorers and the people who helped them.

In the early 1400s, much of the world was a mystery to Europeans. Maps of lands beyond the **horizon** were crude at best. Yet curiosity was fueled by stories told by travelers to the **Far East** and armies returning from war. At the same time, improvements in shipbuilding and **navigation** were making it possible for explorers to travel longer and farther than ever before. It was the dawn of the **Age of Exploration and Discovery**.

WORDS *to* KNOW

horizon: the line in the distance where the land or sea seems to meet the sky.

Far East: area including East and Southeast Asia.

navigation: method of finding your way and figuring out your location.

Age of Exploration and Discovery: a period in history from the early 1400s to the early 1600s, when Europeans explored and mapped the world.

Beginning in the 1400s and lasting into the 1600s, the Age of Discovery was an exciting time for Europe. The kings and queens of Europe sent explorers sailing into the unknown to find new **trading routes**, conquer new lands, or bring back gold. Many times, the explorers got lost and found something completely unexpected.

With each voyage, Europe's knowledge of the world grew. The unknown became clearer as the **New World** was explored and mapped.

# WORDS *to* KNOW

trading route: a route used to carry goods from one place to be sold in another.

New World: North and South America.

legendary: famous.

Americas: the land and islands of North, South, and Central America.

In this book you'll learn about the **legendary** explorers and voyages. You'll learn some history of the time in which the explorers lived and interesting facts about the people and places around them. You'll also read about the discovery of the **Americas**.

Most of the projects in this book can be made with little adult supervision, using materials you already have at home or can easily find at a craft store. So get ready to step back in time and discover the men who were the explorers of the New World and the kings and queens who sent them on their journeys!

Chapter 1

Searching for a Water Route to Asia

In the 1400s, spices, silk, and gold lured European traders east to Asia, a region they called the Indies. Cinnamon, cloves, nutmeg, and pepper were very popular in Europe. Spices preserved meats and made dried foods taste better. They hid the bad taste of spoiled food. These spices grew far to the east of India, on islands called the Spice Islands. In addition to spices, beautiful silk fabrics from China were in high demand throughout Europe.

To reach the Indies, travelers had to journey along the **Silk Road**. This route was thousands of miles long. A single trip on the Silk Road could take years to complete. Along the way, traders had to cross hot deserts and high mountains. They also faced danger from highway **bandits** and countries at war. Traders endured these hardships because Europeans paid a lot of money for silks and spices, making many **merchants** wealthy.

WORDS to KNOW

preserve: to dry, smoke, or salt food so it won't spoil.

Silk Road: the ancient network of trade routes connecting the Mediterranean Sea and China by land.

bandit: a thief.

merchant: someone who buys and sells goods for a profit.

WORDS *to* KNOW

Arabs: a group of people that comes from the Arabian Peninsula.

settlement: a place where a group of people moves to start a new community.

fleet: a group of ships traveling together.

Ottoman Turks: rulers of the Ottoman Empire.

Ottoman Empire: an empire based in Turkey that controlled North Africa, southern Europe, and Southwest Asia.

Exploration Before the Age of Discovery

Before Europe's Age of Discovery, people from other places also explored the world around them.

MIDDLE EAST: Explorers from the Middle East traveled throughout the Persian Gulf, visiting new lands and trading with the people they found there. In 850–851, the **Arab** merchant Suleiman sailed to India, the Spice Islands, Vietnam, and China.

VIKINGS: In the 700s, Vikings from what is now Norway and Sweden discovered Iceland and Greenland. Leif Erikson, one of the most famous Viking explorers, sailed all the way to North America, nearly 500 years before Columbus. Erikson established the first European **settlement** on the continent and named it Vinland. For years, no one knew exactly where Vinland was located. Then, in 1961, the foundations of eight buildings in northern Newfoundland in Canada were uncovered. One was of a large house that looked very much like Erikson's great hall in Greenland. Today, this site is accepted as the place where Erikson built Vinland.

CHINA: In the early 1400s, the Chinese had the largest and fastest **fleet** of ships in the world. Led by seven-foot-tall Admiral Zheng He, the fleet traded with 37 countries in the Persian Gulf, Red Sea, eastern Africa, and along the Vietnam Coast. Some believe Zheng He's explorations reached the Americas during this time, many years before the Europeans. China's domination of the seas ended in 1433, when the Chinese emperor decided that the journeys were too expensive. ∞

SEARCHING FOR A
WATER ROUTE TO ASIA

The Silk Road passed through the city of Constantinople, in present-day Turkey. When the **Ottoman Turks** conquered Constantinople in 1453, they renamed it Istanbul and blocked European travel through their lands. If European merchants wanted to buy valuable spices and silks from the Far East, they had to pay the **Ottoman Empire**. The Europeans needed a new route to Asia.

Because China was east of Europe, some Europeans thought that if they sailed south through the Atlantic Ocean and then east around Africa, they would eventually find a way to the Indies by sea. This new route would be faster and less expensive than the land route. The country that could find this new water route to Asia would have enormous power and wealth from the spice and silk trade. And the explorer who discovered this route? He would become world famous and fantastically rich.

DID YOU KNOW?

During the 15th century, China and Japan were known as Cathay and Cipangu.

ASIA

Istanbul
(Constantinople)

← The Silk Road

EUROPE

CHINA

JAPAN

AFRICA

INDIA

OTTOMAN
EMPIRE

Persian
Gulf

Arabian
Peninsula

Spice
Islands

5

Prince Henry the Navigator

WORDS *to* KNOW

navigator: a person who works to find or direct a route, usually by sea.

cartographer: a person who makes maps.

astronomer: a person who studies the stars, planets, and sky.

geographer: a person who studies the earth's surface and its people, plants, and animals.

Portugal was the country ready to take on this challenge. For most of the fifteenth century, Portugal led the way in sea exploration. It helped that Portugal had a long coastline with many harbors and rivers flowing into the Atlantic Ocean. It also had a powerful royal figure pushing Portugal into unexplored waters. His name was Prince Henry, and he lived from 1394 to 1460.

In 1415, Prince Henry heard stories about great trading centers in East Africa. If he could find a sea route from Portugal to East Africa and the Indies, Portugal could buy spices and silk without having to pay the Ottoman Empire.

To prepare his explorers, Prince Henry established a school of navigation in Sagres, a city on the southwestern tip of Portugal. He gathered an immense collection of books. **Navigators**, ship captains, **cartographers**, instrument makers, **astronomers**, and **geographers** gathered at the school to share their knowledge with others.

Prince Henry (1394–1460)

WORDS to KNOW

maritime: having to do with the sea and sailing.

compass: a device that uses a magnet to show which direction is north.

caravel: a small Portuguese or Spanish sailing ship, usually with triangular sails on two or three masts.

DID YOU KNOW?

Although he was called Prince Henry the Navigator for his efforts to discover a sea route to East Africa and the Indies, Prince Henry never actually sailed on any of the voyages he supported.

These **maritime** scholars improved the **compass** and other tools of navigation. They created better maps. The prince's shipbuilders also designed a new, lighter ship called the **caravel**, which could travel farther and faster.

Prince Henry became convinced that if his captains could sail around Africa, they would find the Indies on the other side. The only problem was that no one knew how far south the continent of Africa went. To find out, Prince Henry started sending ships into the Atlantic Ocean to sail down Africa's west coast.

The captains made maps, charted **currents**, and kept daily written records, called logs, about their voyages. Each captain sailed a little bit farther and reported what he learned to Prince Henry's school. Cartographers revised maps and charts with the new information. Each voyage made the next, longer trip possible.

As Prince Henry's captains sailed down the African coast, they set up **outposts** to trade for gold. They also made contact with the native African people. In 1441, Prince Henry's men began capturing Africans to sell as **slaves**. The Portuguese used profits from the slave trade to help pay for their sea **expeditions**.

WORDS *to* KNOW

current: the movement of water in a river or an ocean.

outpost: a remote settlement.

slave: a person owned by another person and forced to work without pay.

expedition: a long voyage with a goal.

By the time Prince Henry died in 1460, Portuguese explorers had traveled 1,500 miles down the West African coast. They had reached Cape Verde, Sierra Leone, and Cape Palmas in present-day Liberia. Prince Henry's support of exploration made Portugal the early leader in the search for a sea route to the Indies.

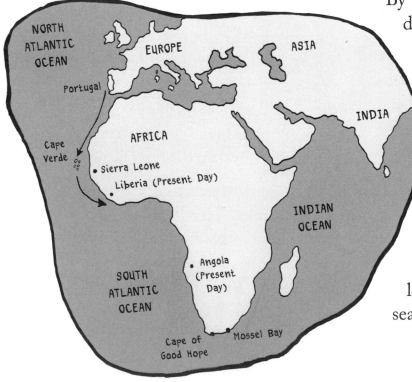

NORTH ATLANTIC OCEAN

EUROPE

ASIA

Portugal

INDIA

AFRICA

Cape Verde

Sierra Leone

Liberia (Present Day)

INDIAN OCEAN

Angola (Present Day)

SOUTH ATLANTIC OCEAN

Cape of Good Hope

Mossel Bay

The Portuguese Caravel

While Prince Henry was developing his navigation school, he decided that the big ships commonly used for ocean voyages, called carracks, were too slow and heavy. Carracks had rectangular sails that worked only when the wind blew from behind. In addition, the carrack had a big, round bottom designed for holding **cargo**, which made it slow.

Prince Henry instructed his shipbuilders to design a new, smaller ship called the caravel. The caravel was slimmer and had a smaller bottom. This gave it greater speed and allowed it to explore in shallow waters. In addition to rectangular sails, the caravel had big triangular sails called **lateen** sails. These were easier to **maneuver** when the wind came from the side or in front of the ship. Sailing along the African coast, Prince Henry's explorers needed to be able to sail no matter which way the wind was blowing.

As voyages became longer, explorers needed bigger ships that held more cargo and crew. By the end of the fifteenth century, caravels were no longer used on expeditions. ∽

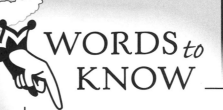

WORDS to KNOW

cargo: goods carried by a ship.

lateen: a triangular sail on a ship.

maneuver: to move something carefully into position.

Bartolomeau Dias

About 20 years later, Prince Henry's great-nephew became king of Portugal. Determined to find the southern tip of Africa, King John II ordered new voyages. He gave the captains of his ships stone pillars called **padrãos**. These pillars had Portugal's coat of arms carved on them. The captains were to place the padrãos along the African coast to claim the land for Portugal.

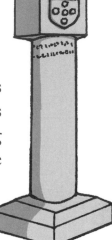

Bartolomeau Dias was one of the men King John sent to find the southern tip of Africa. In August 1487, Dias set sail from Lisbon, Portugal, with two caravels and a supply ship. Dias followed the African coast, passing the **equator** and present-day Angola. In January 1488, Dias sailed into a great storm. Waves tossed the ships and winds drove them south. While the storm raged for 13 days, the frightened sailors lost sight of land. When it was over, the supply ship had disappeared. Without supplies, Dias's crew assumed they would turn around and go home.

WORDS *to* KNOW

padrão: a large stone pillar carved with Portugal's coat of arms. It was placed by explorers to claim land.

equator: an imaginary line around the earth, halfway between the North and South Poles.

Bartolomeau Dias (1457–1500)

Atlantic Slave Trade

Slave trading was a profitable business for Portuguese explorers. Arab traders captured people from the tribes of West Africa and sold them to the Portuguese. From 1441 to 1500, about 50,000 Africans were brought to Portugal. Most Europeans, including the Portuguese, did not respect African people. They thought Africans were primitive and useful only as slaves. In the 1600s, the new American colonies needed workers for their sugar and tobacco plantations. The demand for slaves grew. European slave traders shipped millions of African people across the Atlantic Ocean to colonies throughout the Americas. ∿

Instead of giving up, however, Dias studied the sun and his charts. He turned the fleet east, thinking he would find land and calm his crew. When he only found more water, Dias realized that the storm must have blown him past the tip of Africa. He changed direction and ordered his ships to sail north. On February 3, 1488, the men spotted land. They **anchored** the ships in Mossel Bay, about 230 miles (370 kilometers) east of the present-day city of Cape Town on Africa's southern tip. Dias placed a padrão in the ground to claim the land for Portugal.

WORDS to KNOW

anchor: to lower a heavy metal hook to the ocean floor to stop a ship from drifting.

Dias wanted to follow the eastern coast farther, but his men were tired of the journey. Their supplies were low and the coastline seemed endless. The sailors and officers threatened **mutiny** if Dias did not turn the ships around and head home to Portugal. Reluctantly, Dias agreed and sailed back to Lisbon.

WORDS *to* KNOW

mutiny: a rebellion of the ship's crew against its captain.

passage: a sea route.

On the return trip, Dias saw the southern tip of Africa, which he had missed earlier because of the storm. He called it the Cape of Storms because of the fierce weather he had encountered. Dias erected another padrão, claiming the **passage** to the Indian Ocean for Portugal.

This area would later become Cape Town, the capital of South Africa.

In December 1488, Dias returned to Lisbon and reported his discoveries to the king. The Cape of Storms was renamed the Cape of Good Hope. King John II felt confident that Dias's discovery was the beginning of Portugal's sea route to the Indies.

DID YOU KNOW?

Bartolomeau Dias died in 1500 when his ship was lost in a violent storm.

Vasco da Gama

Not long after Dias returned, King John II died. The new king was Manuel I. He heard that by sailing west, Christopher Columbus had discovered a string of islands, the Bahamas, and claimed them for Spain. Not to be outdone by his Spanish rivals, King Manuel decided to send another explorer to find the sea route all the way to the Indies.

King Manuel chose a Portuguese navigator named Vasco da Gama to lead the expedition. Da Gama set sail on July 8, 1497 with 4 ships and about 170 men. Each ship had guns, **crossbows**, javelins, **pikes**, and spears for defense. Spectators crowded around the docks to wave goodbye to the brave man who were expected to bring glory and treasure to Portugal.

WORDS to KNOW

crossbow: a weapon used to shoot arrows.

pike: a long wooden pole with a steel head.

Vasco da Gama (1469–1524)

Da Gama decided not to follow the African coast closely, as earlier explorers had done. Instead, he headed away from the coast and into the Atlantic Ocean. This route took advantage of the sea winds and currents, helping the ships to sail faster. In fact, this route is still used today by ships sailing from Europe to Africa's southern tip.

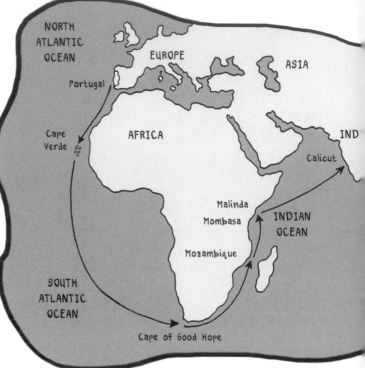

About five months after leaving Portugal, da Gama arrived at the Cape of Good Hope. His ships rounded Africa's southern tip, then sailed up the east coast toward India.

Along the way, da Gama found foods he had never seen before—melons, cucumbers, and coconuts.

He stopped in Mozambique, a country on Africa's southeastern coast. There he found ship captains were great knowledge, clever merchants, and people dressed in fine silks and linens. In Mombasa, a city in present-day Kenya, da Gama arrived at a harbor filled with ships from ports along the Indian Ocean. The fleet continued north, reaching Malindi (also in Kenya) by mid-April.

Marco Polo

Marco Polo (1254–1324) was born into a family of merchants from Venice, Italy. He was one of the greatest early explorers. When Polo was 17 years old, his father and uncle took him on a trading journey to the Far East. They followed the Silk Road all the way to China. Marco Polo became a favorite with China's ruler, the Khan, and served in his court. He was sent on several special missions in China, Burma, and India. Polo finally returned home to Venice 24 years after he left!

A master of several languages, Marco Polo was gifted at understanding cultures different from his own. He traveled thousands of miles through deserts and steep mountain passes. He faced extreme weather and wild animals. His writings about his trips and adventures became one of the world's greatest **travelogues**. It opened the door to the East for thousands of travelers from the West. ∾

WORDS *to* KNOW

travelogue: a written account of a journey or travels.

In Malindi, da Gama found a pilot to guide him across the Indian Ocean to India. On May 20, 1498, Vasco da Gama anchored in Calicut, India (now called Kozhikode). Da Gama erected a padrão to prove he had finally reached this far-off land. Calicut was the most important trading center in southern India. The local Hindu king, the Zamorin, welcomed the Portuguese explorers.

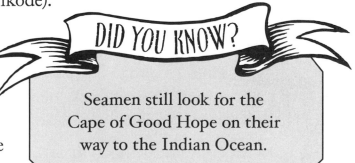

DID YOU KNOW?

Seamen still look for the Cape of Good Hope on their way to the Indian Ocean.

WORDS *to* KNOW

scurvy: a disease common among sailors, caused by the lack of vitamin C in the diet. Vitamin C is found in fruits like oranges.

pension: an amount of money paid at regular times for past service.

Admiral: a high rank in the navy that places a person in charge of a fleet of ships.

rival: a person or group that competes with another.

DID YOU KNOW?

The meeting of the Atlantic and Indian Oceans at the Cape of Good Hope creates powerful waves and currents that can sink ships.

Da Gama hoped to reach a trade agreement with the Hindu king. But the Portuguese gifts of cheap striped fabric and coral beads insulted the king and his men. The king was used to receiving lavish gifts of gold from traders. When da Gama presented the Zamorin with a letter from King Manuel requesting a trade agreement between the two countries, the Zamorin refused. He ordered da Gama to leave Calicut immediately.

With a load of spices, da Gama sailed back across the Indian Ocean. The journey home was long and hard. More than half of the men died of **scurvy**. So many died that da Gama burned one of the ships because he did not have enough men to sail it. Finally, on July 10, 1499, the fleet arrived in Portugal, two years after its departure.

King Manuel was pleased at da Gama's successful voyage to the Indies. He rewarded the explorer with two **pensions** and granted him the title of Dom and **Admiral** of India. Da Gama sailed on two more expeditions to India, in 1502 and 1524. During his third expedition, da Gama became ill in India and died there.

The efforts of men like Prince Henry the Navigator, Bartolomeau Dias, and Vasco da Gama, sparked a great wave of European maritime exploration. Dias's discovery of Africa's southern tip and da Gama's voyage to India proved that a sea route around Africa to the Indies was possible. Their discoveries started a race among European nations to explore new sea routes and claim new lands. Portugal's neighbor, Spain, would quickly become one of its biggest **rivals** in the race to trade with the Indies.

Pedro Álvares Cabral

After Vasco da Gama returned from India in 1499, King Manuel I of Portugal planned a larger voyage back to India. Pedro Álvares Cabral, a member of the King's Council, was chosen to lead the fleet of 13 ships. On March 19, 1500, Cabral's fleet sailed for India. Cabral planned to take the same route that da Gama had followed. But a storm forced Cabral's fleet off course, blowing them far to the west. On April 22, Cabral's crew sighted land. Without knowing it, Cabral's ship had crossed the Atlantic and reached the eastern tip of South America! He became the first European in recorded history to land on the coast of what is now Brazil. ∿

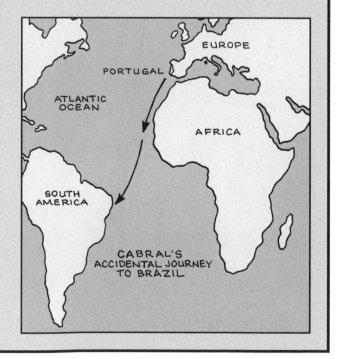

latitude: the position of a place, measured in degrees north or south of the equator.

North Star: the brightest star in the **Northern Hemisphere**. It is at the end of the handle of the Little Dipper.

Northern Hemisphere: the half of the earth north of the equator.

SUPPLIES

- ⅄ file folder
- ⅄ scissors
- ⅄ wooden yardstick
- ⅄ rubber bands
- ⅄ wooden 1-foot ruler
- ⅄ notebook
- ⅄ pencil

MAKE YOUR OWN CROSS STAFF

Sailors in the fifteenth century used the cross staff to find their **latitude**. This tool measured the height of the **North Star** or the sun above the horizon. The higher the North Star, the farther north the ship was.

1 Cut a 2-by-6-inch strip (5 by 15 centimeters) from the file folder. Wrap the strip tightly around the yardstick.

2 Wrap a rubber band around the strip on the yardstick so that the strip is able to slide on the yardstick, but not shift when in place.

3 Spread two turns of the rubber band to form an "X" and carefully push the ruler through the "X". The ruler should be perpendicular to the yardstick. The "X" should be close to the center of the crosspiece.

4 To use your cross staff, hold it so the ruler is vertical and the yardstick is horizontal. Place one end of the yardstick just below your eye. Point the other end toward the horizon. Slide the cross-piece toward or away from you until its upper edge lines up with the sun and the lower edge lines up with the horizon. Write down where the ruler stops on the yardstick. Do this at 8 a.m., noon, 4 p.m., and sunset.

CLASSROOM CONNECTION: Bring your notebook and cross staff to class and teach your classmates to use it.

MAKE YOUR OWN SPICE MIXES

For thousands of years, Europeans have used Old World spices such as black pepper, cinnamon, ginger, nutmeg, and cloves. Spices preserved meats, made dried foods taste better, and hid the bad taste of spoiled food. Spices were used for medicines, too.

Discovery of the New World gave Europeans new spices, such as chili peppers, vanilla, and allspice. Try seasoning meat, chicken, or fish with these spice mixes and see how they taste. Or, you can stir some into a dollop of sour cream, dip in a chip, and see which one you like better!

1 Measure and combine all the ingredients in a mixing bowl. Stir to mix thoroughly.

2 Pour your spice mixes into glass jars or other airtight containers. Store in a cool, dry place.

MEAT RUB RECIPE:
1 Tablespoon salt, 1 bay leaf, 2 Tablespoons white pepper, 2 Tablespoons black pepper, 1 teaspoon nutmeg, 1 teaspoon cinnamon, 1 Tablespoon allspice, 1 Tablespoon mace, 1 Tablespoon cloves

BARBECUE SEASONING RECIPE:
2 Tablespoons paprika, $\frac{1}{2}$ teaspoon curry powder, 1 Tablespoon chili powder, $\frac{1}{2}$ teaspoon dry mustard, 1 teaspoon ground coriander, $\frac{1}{2}$ teaspoon black pepper, 1 teaspoon sugar

SUPPLIES

Y mixing bowl

Y measuring spoons

Y assorted spices (*see recipes to left*)

Y stirring spoon

Y small glass or plastic jars with tight-fitting lids

MAKE YOUR OWN LOG BOOK

Sailors used log books to record details of their journeys. They often shared these records with other explorers when they returned home.

1 On the construction paper or cardstock, use a black or colored marker to make a front and back cover for your log book. Add decorations or drawings to your cover. Punch three holes into the side of your cover.

2 Punch three holes into a stack of lined paper. Sandwich the paper between the two cover pages. Push a piece of yarn or string through each hole and tie in a double knot.

3 Take your log book the next time you travel and record your observations. What do you see? What is the weather like? What direction are you traveling? How long does it take you to arrive?

SUPPLIES

- Y 2 pieces of heavy paper like construction paper or cardstock
- Y black or colored marker
- Y pencil
- Y 3-hole punch
- Y several sheets of lined paper
- Y 3 pieces yarn, each 8 inches long (20 centimeters)

CLASSROOM CONNECTION:
Take your log book on your next class trip. Record everything you see and do on the trip. When you return, share your observations with your class.

SHiP Log book

MAKE YOUR OWN
Clay Padrãos

When Portuguese explorers explored new land, they often erected stone. These padrãos carried Portugal's coat of arms to show that they claimed the land for Portugal.

1 Mix cornstarch, baking soda, and water in a saucepan. Cook the mixture over medium heat, stirring regularly until it stiffens into a clay-like consistency. Be patient, this takes a few minutes. When the clay is stiff, spoon it onto a large piece of waxed paper.

2 When the clay is cool enough to touch, knead it until smooth. Add a few drops of food coloring and knead until well mixed.

3 Think of symbols that represent you and your family. Your symbols can be of animals, sports, or even the first letter of your name. Set aside some clay to make your symbols.

4 Roll the rest of the clay into a pillar shape. Make the bottom wide enough to support one main symbol. Form your symbol and attach it to the top of your pillar.

5 You can engrave other symbols or words on the body of the pillar, just as the Portuguese placed their coat of arms on their padrãos. Let your padrãos harden for 24 hours.

CLASSROOM CONNECTION: Share your padrãos with your class. Explain how the symbols you chose to decorate the padrãos represent your family.

SUPPLIES

- 1 cup cornstarch
- 2 cups baking soda
- $1\frac{1}{4}$ cups water
- saucepan
- spoon
- stove
- waxed paper
- food coloring (optional)

Chapter 2

Voyage to the New World, Christopher Columbus

While the Portuguese explored the African coast for a passage east to the Indies, another explorer was determined to sail a different way—west!

Christopher Columbus (1451–1506)

Christopher Columbus is one of the most famous explorers in the world. He was born Cristoforo Colombo in Genoa in 1451. Today, Genoa is part of Italy. In Columbus's time, Genoa was an independent state and a wealthy trading center.

Very little is known about Columbus's childhood. He must have been educated. He read ancient Greek and Roman stories and could speak several languages by the time he was an adult.

WORDS to KNOW

harbor: a place where ships shelter or unload their cargo.

mariner: sailor.

At age 15, Columbus left home to go to sea. He worked on trading ships that crossed the Mediterranean Sea. During this time, he learned sailing and navigational skills.

In 1476, pirates off the coast of Portugal attacked the ship Columbus was sailing on. When his ship burned and sank, an injured Columbus swam to the Portuguese shore.

After Columbus recovered, he joined his brother Bartholomew in Lisbon, Portugal. The city was a busy seaport. Its **harbor** held many ships that traveled up and down the west coast of Africa. Christopher found a job at the mapmaking shop where Bartholomew worked. There he learned the skills of mapmaking. He also listened to **mariners** talk about their sea adventures and the places they had been. Columbus read Marco Polo's book about his travels to China. All of these stories must have stirred a tremendous yearning to explore.

Eager for his own adventures, Columbus sailed from Lisbon on long merchant voyages north to Ireland and south down the west coast of Africa. On these trips, he learned about Atlantic currents that flowed east and west.

By the late 1400s, Portugal was buzzing with excitement about exploration. Dias had just returned from finding the tip of Africa in 1488. The lure of fame and fortune sent many more adventurers down the coast of Africa, looking for the sea route to the Indies. Columbus had a different idea. He thought there might be another shortcut to the Indies. He planned to sail straight across the Ocean Sea.

In Columbus's time, the Atlantic Ocean was known as the Ocean Sea or the Sea of Darkness. The cold, dark waters seemed to stretch endlessly west. A voyage across the Ocean Sea would probably take years to complete. Any ship attempting such a crossing would certainly run out of food, water, or become lost at sea before finding land.

While educated people knew that the earth was a **sphere**, no one knew that the Americas lay across the Ocean Sea.

Columbus studied maps of the world. He estimated the distance between the Canary Islands (off the northwest coast of Africa) and Japan to be about 2,300 miles (3,701 kilometers). China should be another 1,500 miles (2,414 kilometers) farther, he thought.

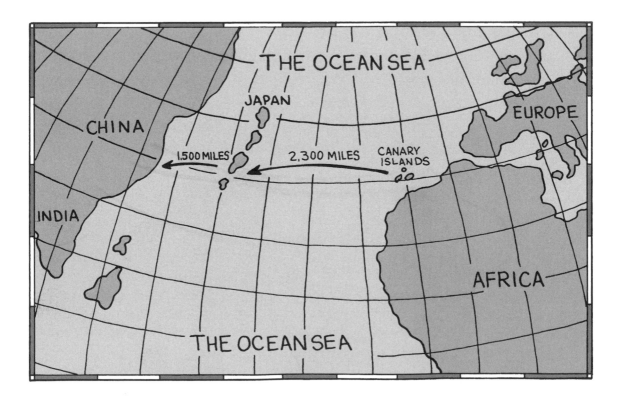

WORDS to KNOW

sphere: round, like a ball.

sponsor: to give money and support.

devout: deeply religious.

convert: to change a person's religious beliefs.

Moors: people from North Africa.

Armed with these calculations, Columbus was convinced that a sea route westward across the Ocean Sea to the Indies would be quicker and safer than trying to round Africa. Now he needed money, ships, and men to prove it. First, he went to King John of Portugal and presented his plan. But King John turned him down, preferring to send ships around the tip of Africa.

So Columbus packed his bags and headed for Spain. Columbus hoped that King Ferdinand V and Queen Isabella I would agree to **sponsor** his voyage. The queen was a **devout** Christian and Columbus thought she would view his voyage as a way to **convert** more people to Christianity.

Columbus traveled to the city of Cordoba, Spain, where the king and queen lived. But the queen was very busy and it took Columbus nine months to meet with her. When he finally explained his idea to the queen, she told him to wait. Spain was in the middle of a war with the **Moors** and did not have the time or money to sponsor Columbus's voyage.

So Columbus waited.
And waited . . .

DID YOU KNOW?

King Ferdinand and Queen Isabella believed that everyone in Spain should be Christians. They set up the Spanish Inquisition to look for and punish people who were not practicing Christians.

Six long years passed and Columbus was no closer to reaching the Indies. Finally, in 1492, the Spanish conquered the Moors. Columbus was excited, but also angry about how long he had waited. He told King Ferdinand and Queen Isabella that he wanted to be called "Admiral of the Ocean Sea." Columbus demanded 10 percent of all the riches he brought back for Spain. The king and queen agreed to Columbus's demands and granted him three ships. The queen reminded Columbus to bring back gold for Spain, and to spread Christianity.

Columbus chose three ships: the *Niña*, the *Pinta*, and the *Santa María*. He commanded the *Santa María*, the largest and slowest of the three ships. It was difficult to convince sailors to sign on for the voyage, because Columbus was a foreigner and many were afraid of sailing into the unknown Sea of Darkness. The search ended when Martín Pinzón, a famous Spanish navigator, signed on for the expedition. Pinzón would command the *Pinta* and his brother Vicente Yáñez agreed to command the *Niña*. Once the brothers were onboard, Columbus easily recruited crew for his ships. On August 3, 1492, Columbus stood on the *Santa María* and gave the order for the fleet to depart.

WORDS *to* KNOW

quadrant: an instrument to measure the height of the planets, moon, or stars.

celestial: to do with the sky or the heavens.

rigging: the ropes and wires on a ship that support and control the sails.

astrolabe: an instrument used to measure the height of celestial bodies above the horizon.

Early Navigational Instruments

During the fifteenth century, sailors had only a few crude instruments, like the cross staff, to help them determine where they were and which direction they were going. For many years, sailors simply hugged the coast, keeping land in sight. But as explorers traveled farther out to sea, they needed better instruments.

The **quadrant** measured the angle of the North Star or the noontime sun from the horizon. Every star has a **celestial** latitude. A sailor could measure the angle between the star and the horizon. Using this angle, a ship's navigator could calculate his latitude. This is the distance in degrees north or south the ship was from the equator. This simple instrument was usually a heavy metal plate in the shape of a quarter of a circle, marked in degrees. It had a lead weight on a string that marked the angle. The navigator would hang the quadrant in the **rigging**, find the sun or North Star along the quadrant's edge and use the weighted string to mark the angle.

The **astrolabe** was another instrument used to measure the height of celestial bodies like the sun or stars above the horizon. It was a heavy brass ring fitted with a double-ended pointer that pivoted at the ring's center. Sailors hung an astrolabe from a cord so that it hung perpendicular to the ship's deck. The navigator spotted the sun or a star through two small holes on the astrolabe's pointer. The altitude of the sun or star spotted was read from a graduated scale around the ring.

The compass gave mariners a rough idea of which direction was north. Some of the earliest compasses used a magnetic stone called a lodestone. The lodestone was shaped like a spoon and rested on a wooden square marked with directions. The handle of the spoon always pointed south. North was opposite. ∾

The First Voyage

Columbus must have been thrilled to be finally on the voyage he had dreamed of for so long. He decided to keep a log. He wrote down the direction of the winds, the cloud patterns, and the distances his ships traveled daily. He used maps and compasses and studied the stars. The first days were clear sailing—the ships covered approximately 850 miles (1,367 kilometers) according to Columbus's calculations.

WORDS *to* KNOW

quarters: living space.

But the voyage lasted longer than Columbus had planned. Day after day passed and no one saw land. On September 18, Martín Pinzón drew the *Pinta* near the *Santa María* and told Columbus that he had seen land the night before. He urged Columbus to change his course from west to north. Columbus refused. He was convinced that there was no large landmass to the north of their position. He would keep heading west, toward Japan. Unhappy, the sailors grew restless. Some rumbled that they would like to throw Columbus overboard.

A Sailor's Life at Sea

Life at sea was not a breeze. In fact, most sailors' lives were very hard. They frequently died from disease, hunger, and thirst. On Columbus's ship, the sailors' day began with prayers and hymns. Then the crew worked in four-hour shifts. Some pumped dirty water that collected in the lowest compartment on the ship. Others cleaned decks, worked sails, and checked ropes and cargo. At the end of the day, there were more religious services. At night, the crew had to search for an open corner to sleep in. Even Columbus did not have private sleeping **quarters** on his own ship! ∾

On September 25, Pinzón again shouted that he had seen land. After so long at sea, sailors on all three ships climbed the rigging to look. They too, swore that there was a distant shore. This time Columbus changed course and headed southwest toward the sighted land. At sunrise, however, they realized that it was really a bunch of storm clouds.

Once again, Columbus set the course for due west. By October, there was still no sight of land. The men drew close to their breaking point. They threatened mutiny.

In his log, Columbus wrote that ". . . they could stand it no longer. I reproached them for their lack of spirit."

Columbus was certain that land was close. Flocks of birds flew overhead, a sure sign that land was near. Holding the angry men back with a gun, Columbus convinced the sailors to give him three more days.

The next day, the sailors spotted more signs of land. A carved branch floated by and more flocks of seagulls flew overhead. That night, Columbus looked to the west and saw a light. At 2 o'clock in the morning, a sailor on the *Pinta* finally spotted land.

DID YOU KNOW?

When Columbus's crew spotted land, his sailors rejoiced and sang the hymn, "Salve, Regina"

Columbus anchored his ships off the strange new land at dawn on October 12. On shore, they planted the Spanish flag and said a prayer of thanksgiving. Columbus claimed the land for Spain and declared its people to be Spanish subjects.

The land's **native people** must have wondered who were these strangely dressed men from the sea? Columbus wrote that "we saw naked people" on shore and that "to some of them I gave red caps, and glass beads which they put on their chests, and many other things of small value, in which they took so much pleasure and became so much our friends that it was a marvel." In return, the natives gave the sailors parrots, spears, and balls of cotton.

It did not occur to Columbus or other European explorers that they did not have the right to take the land. In fact, Columbus's attitude was typical of many Europeans. He wrote about the native people, "They ought to make good and skilled servants."

Through it all, Columbus believed that he had reached an outlying island in the Indies. Columbus named the island San Salvador, which means "Holy Savior" in Spanish. Instead of the Indies, however, Columbus had really discovered an island in the Bahamas.

WORDS *to* KNOW

native people: people with their own culture who live in an area before anyone arrives from another country.

Eager to find Japan, and gold, Columbus set sail again two days later. Sailing from island to island, he looked for the riches of Asia that Marco Polo had described in his book. He took native guides on board with him. Everywhere he landed, he found rich, tropical landscapes and friendly natives. Columbus was amazed by the New World's surroundings.

"All of the trees are as different from ours as day is from night. And so are the fruits, the herbage, the rocks, and everything," he wrote.

Despite his efforts, Columbus did not find Japan or gold. The natives spoke of an island they called Colba, which was present-day Cuba. But when Columbus arrived at the large island on October 28, he quickly realized it was not Japan.

By November 1492, Martín Pinzón, the captain of the *Pinta*, had tired of following Columbus. He decided to strike out on his own and search for gold. He sailed the *Pinta* away from the fleet. Columbus was very angry, but decided to continue his journey without Pinzón.

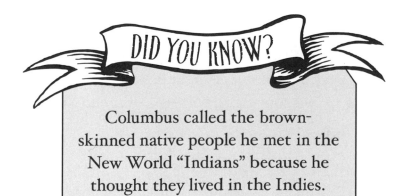

DID YOU KNOW?

Columbus called the brown-skinned native people he met in the New World "Indians" because he thought they lived in the Indies.

WORDS *to* KNOW

reef: a strip of rock or coral close to the surface of the water.

Left with two ships, Columbus explored more islands searching for gold. On December 6, Columbus landed on an island that is present-day Haiti and the Dominican Republic. He named the beautiful island Hispaniola, because it reminded him of Spain. "Our Lord in his mercy direct me until I find the gold mine. I have many people here who say that they know where it is," he wrote.

Unfortunately, the *Santa María* hit a coral **reef** on Christmas Eve. The crew tried to save the ship, but it began to sink. Columbus and his crew moved the supplies and used the ship's timbers to build a fort on the island of Hispaniola. Forty men would stay at the fort, named La Navidad, while Columbus sailed back to Spain for more ships.

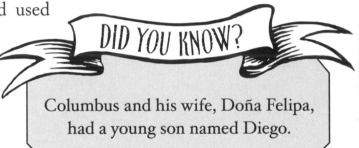

DID YOU KNOW?

Columbus and his wife, Doña Felipa, had a young son named Diego.

On January 4, 1493, Columbus boarded the *Niña* and set sail for home. As he headed east, he feared that Martín Pinzón would beat him back to Spain and steal his glory. Two days later, however, Martín Pinzón surprised Columbus by reappearing with the *Pinta* to join him for the return voyage to Spain.

"I do not know why he has been so disloyal and untrustworthy toward me," Columbus wrote in his log. "Even so, I am going to ignore these actions."

Treaty of Tordesillas

King John of Portugal and Queen Isabella of Spain wanted to determine which new lands could be claimed by Spain and which ones could be claimed by Portugal. They asked the Pope, Alexander VI, to decide. The Pope chose a line west of the Cape Verde Islands that ran from the North to the South Pole. All lands discovered to the west of that line would belong to Spain. All lands found east of the line would belong to Portugal. An agreement was signed by Spain and Portugal in 1494, called the Treaty of Tordesillas. In 1506, the agreement was changed to move the line 1,185 miles (1,907 kilometers) farther west of the Cape Verde Islands. This allowed Portugal to claim the coast of Brazil. ∾

On March 15, 1493, Columbus arrived in Palos, Spain. He paraded through the country, making his way to see the king and queen in Barcelona. When he reached the court, the king and queen gave him a royal welcome. Word quickly spread throughout Spain that the Admiral of the Ocean Sea had found the Indies!

Columbus presented the king and queen with green parrots, gold objects, and several natives. He told them the story of his expedition and discoveries. Everywhere he went, people were thrilled to hear the great explorer's stories. Soon all of Europe was fascinated by his discoveries.

The Second Voyage

WORDS to KNOW

colonize: to settle in another country.

colonist: someone who settles a new area.

bullying: forcing someone to do what you want or treating a weaker person badly.

retaliate: to fight back.

Ferdinand and Isabella wanted to **colonize** the newly discovered lands for Spain. This time Columbus had no trouble gathering a fleet and crew for the return journey. He assembled 17 ships at Cadiz and more than 1,200 men, including sailors, **colonists**, soldiers, and priests.

On September 25, 1493, Columbus and his fleet left Cadiz amid celebrations. This time the journey across the ocean was smooth. After anchoring off the coast of Hispaniola, Columbus shot flares of greeting towards the fort he had left behind. But no one responded. On the island, Columbus and his men found the fort burned and all the men killed. A local chief told Columbus that the men left behind grew greedy and fought among themselves. Several began **bullying** the natives, looking for women and gold. A group of natives **retaliated** and wiped out the fort.

This violent incident would set the pattern for unfriendly relations between native people and European explorers for years to come.

WORDS *to* KNOW

resource: anything to help people take care of themselves, such as water, food, and building materials.

quest: a search for something.

Filled with sadness, Columbus sailed east along the coast of Hispaniola and anchored at a new spot. There he founded a town named La Isabela after the Spanish queen. Columbus spent several months building the settlement and exploring the island.

In April 1494, Columbus left his brother Diego in charge of La Isabela and sailed for Cuba. But he did not discover gold or Asia. Not wanting to admit failure, Columbus ordered his men to sign a document and swear that Cuba was so large it must be part of China.

Returning to La Isabela, Columbus found that his brother had done a terrible job leading the colonists, who were angry. Columbus realized he had picked a poor location for La Isabela. It sat in a swampy, mosquito-filled area with few **resources** and a bad harbor.

In his **quest** for gold, Columbus became convinced that the native people knew where to find it. He ordered natives over the age of 14 to deliver a bell filled with gold every three months. If they did

DID YOU KNOW?

At the Panama Canal, the southern settlement is named Cristóbal, after Christopher Columbus.

not, the penalty would be death. They were also forced to supply the Spanish with food. Many natives died at the hands of the Spanish through violence, overwork, or disease. Some colonists were so upset with how Columbus was governing La Isabela that they returned to Spain. Once home, they sharply criticized Columbus to the king and queen.

Eventually, Columbus decided to return to Spain. He wanted to defend his actions to the crown and ask for more help establishing the colony. He left his brothers, Bartholomew and Diego, in charge of La Isabela. Setting sail on March 10, 1496, Columbus arrived off the coast of Portugal on June 8.

WORDS to KNOW

criminal: a person who has committed a crime.

mainland: the land of a continent.

The Third Voyage

Despite Columbus's failure to find gold on his first two voyages, Ferdinand and Isabela granted his request for a third voyage. This time, Columbus sailed from southern Spain on May 30, 1498 with six ships. The complaints of the unhappy colonists made recruiting for this voyage difficult. Columbus was forced to take some **criminals**, people who took the work because they had no other options.

When they left Spain, the fleet split into two groups. Three ships sailed to Hispaniola with supplies. Columbus led the other three ships on a mission to find Asia's **mainland** and its riches.

How America Got Its Name

In 1497, an Italian named Amerigo Vespucci sailed to the New World. He realized that it was not Asia, but a brand new land. A few years later, in 1507, a German mapmaker mistakenly credited Vespucci with discovering the new continents. As a result, he gave the name Amerigo to the northern and southern continents. They eventually became known as North and South America. ∾

On this voyage, Columbus made landfall on an island with three peaks, which he named Trinidad. Then he sailed to the coast of Venezuela, becoming the first European to see South America. But Columbus's health was poor, and he ordered the ships to sail for Hispaniola.

WORDS *to* **KNOW**

revolt: to fight against a government or person of authority.

Columbus found the colony in chaos. The lack of gold disappointed the colonists, who **revolted** against Columbus. More complaints flowed back to the royal courts against Columbus and his brother.

In 1500, the king and queen sent a royal governor to inspect the situation. When the governor arrived, he found conditions so bad that Columbus was arrested and sent back to Spain in chains.

For the aging explorer, it was quite a different return from the celebrations that greeted him after his first voyage.

The Final Voyage

The proud explorer was anxious to restore his good name. Traveling around Africa and then east, Vasco da Gama had already reached the Indies for Portugal. If Spain was to find her own riches, they would have to use Columbus's route to the west. But where was the path through the islands to the rich Indies? Columbus still believed he could find it. He convinced Ferdinand and Isabela to give him one more chance.

On May 9, 1502, Columbus set sail for the fourth and final time, with four ships headed to the New World. The queen told Columbus not to land in Hispaniola, because he would not be welcome.

Columbus found present-day Central America and searched for a passage to the East. But storms drenched the crew, the food spoiled, worms ate the ship's timber, and everyone's spirits fell. Columbus himself was sick. He knew if he did not find a path to the East on this trip, it would be his last.

Fighting poor eyesight, bad health, and rotting ships, Columbus finally decided to head to Hispaniola and then home. But before he could reach the colony, a storm blew him off course and stranded him on Jamaica. The ships were so badly damaged they could not sail without repairs. So Columbus sent men in canoes to Hispaniola for rescue. The colony's new governor, however, delayed sending help. The governor made him wait a year for rescue.

For the last time, Columbus sailed back to Spain and settled with his son in Seville. He spent much of his final days seeking to restore his titles and riches.

Until his death in May 1506, Columbus was convinced that he had reached the Indies. He never knew that he had really discovered a whole New World!

WORDS *to* KNOW

longitude: lines perpendicular to the equator, measuring distance east or west from a point in England.

DID YOU KNOW?

During the Age of Exploration, navigators did not have a tool to measure their **longitude** at sea. They had to use dead reckoning to figure out where they were. Dead reckoning was a method of navigation. Sailors figured out a ship's position by calculating its speed, sailing time, and direction.

A Glimpse of the Pacific Ocean

Inspired by Columbus, a Spaniard named Vasco Nuñez de Balboa sailed to the New World in 1500. After years of exploration, he founded a colony named *Santa María* de l'Antiqua del Darién in present-day Columbia.

In 1513, Balboa heard stories about a new sea. He organized an expedition and headed south. When the group reached the narrow piece of land that is present-day Panama, they set off through dense rainforests heading west. On September 25, Balboa climbed a mountain and became the first European to view the eastern shores of the great Pacific Ocean. When they reached the shore, he claimed the sea and all the land that touched it for Spain. ∾

MAKE YOUR OWN COMPASS

Before to the compass, sailors used landmarks and the position of the sun and stars to tell them which direction to sail. They often kept within sight of land, in case it became foggy or cloudy. The invention of the compass allowed sailors to navigate safely away from land. A compass's magnetized needle aligns itself with the lines of the earth's magnetic field. When the compass is level, the needle turns until one end points to the North magnetic pole, giving sailors direction no matter what the weather.

SUPPLIES

- ❦ small paper clip, straightened
- ❦ magnet
- ❦ small piece of Styrofoam (packing peanuts work great)
- ❦ bowl of water
- ❦ permanent marker

1 Rub the straightened paper clip with the magnet for several minutes. Push the paper clip all the way through the Styrofoam.

2 Gently place the paper clip and Styrofoam on the surface of water. Allow the needle enough time to align along the magnetic fields of the earth. It will then point north. If you gently blow on the needle, the same end of the needle should always return to the same direction.

3 Mark the north end of the needle with permanent marker.

CLASSROOM CONNECTION: Take your compass to different points in your school. Which direction is north?

LEARN ALL ABOUT
LATITUDE AND LONGITUDE

You can tell where you are on the globe if you know your latitude and longitude.

1 Latitude is the distance a point is from the equator. The equator is a line around the center of the earth that is an equal distance from both poles. All lines of latitude are parallel to the equator. Latitude tells you how far above or below the equator you are.

2 Lines of longitude run perpendicular to the equator. Each line of longitude is part of a circle that goes around the entire globe and passes through both poles. The earth is divided into 360 degrees of longitude. The line that has the value of zero degrees is called the Prime Meridian. It goes through Greenwich, England. All other lines of longitude are measured east and west of the Prime Meridian. Knowing your longitude will tell you how far east or west of the Prime Meridian you are.

3 Looking at your globe or map, find what continents are at the following latitudes and longitudes. Write your answers on a piece of paper and check your navigational skills at the end!

a. Latitude 15°N, longitude 30°W
b. Latitude 45°N, longitude 105°W
c. Latitude 30°S, longitude 135°W
d. Latitude 15°N, longitude 60°W
e. Latitude 45°N, longitude 15°W
f. Latitude 30°N, longitude 90°W

SUPPLIES

- globe or map of the earth with latitude and longitude lines
- pencil
- paper

a. Africa, b. North America, c. Australia, d. South America, e. Europe, f. Asia.

ANSWER KEY:

41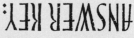

MAKE YOUR OWN QUADRANT

A quadrant is a simple instrument that sailors used to measure the height above the horizon of the sun and stars. Held vertically and aligned with a sun or star, a weighted string fell across a scale marked with degrees. This indicated the object's angle above the horizon.

SUPPLIES

- ᛉ quadrant template (*see next page*)
- ᛉ scissors
- ᛉ glue
- ᛉ lightweight cardboard, cereal box, or a file folder
- ᛉ straw
- ᛉ tape
- ᛉ string
- ᛉ large bead or paperclip

1 Make a copy of the quadrant template. Cut out the copied quadrant and glue it to a piece of cardboard or file folder. Cut the quadrant and its backing out with scissors.

2 Glue or tape your straw to the back of the quadrant so that it is parallel with the straight edge of the quadrant that starts at "0."

3 Make a small hole through the corner of the quadrant. Tie a knot in the string or tape it to secure it to the quadrant. Tie a bead or paperclip to the other end of the string. This will act as the weight.

4 To use your quadrant, wait until night and pick a bright star in the sky. With the arc of the quadrant facing you, look along the straight edge through the straw. Line up the star through the straw so that it looks as if it is touching the end of the quadrant. Let the string hang down and then hold it in place. Read the number on the arc. This is the height of the star in degrees. Remember that stars will be in different places in the sky depending on the time of night and how far north or south you are.

TRACE-IT TEMPLATE QUADRANT

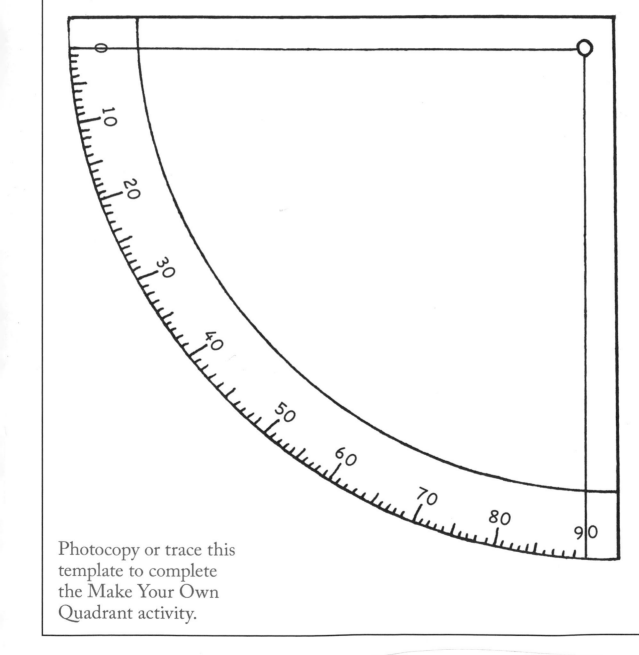

10
20
30
40
50
60
70
80
90

Photocopy or trace this template to complete the Make Your Own Quadrant activity.

MAKE YOUR OWN MAP QUEST

With each expedition, explorers improved and added to maps of the New World. Later, explorers used these maps to travel to the New World.

SUPPLIES

Y paper
Y pencil
Y ruler
Y spice bag from Chapter 1 activity or other item for "treasure"

1 Draw a map of your school or home on a piece of paper. Using your ruler, add lines of longitude and latitude to the map, about 1 inch apart (2½ centimeters). Label the center horizontal line 0 degrees. Label the horizontal lines above the center line in increments of 10 degrees and "N" for North (i.e. 10 degrees N, 20 degrees N, 30 degrees N). Repeat for the horizontal lines below the center, beginning again at 10 degrees, but labeling each line "S" for South.

2 Label the center vertical line as 0 degrees. Label the vertical lines in 10-degree increments, making the lines to the right ("East") and the lines to the left ("West").

3 Hide your spice bag or treasure somewhere in the school or home.

4 Write directions to the bag using only latitude and longitude coordinates from your map. See who can find the bag first!

treasure = 40° w, 20° N

Chapter 3

Searching for the Northwest Passage, John Cabot

When Christopher Columbus returned from his first voyage across the Atlantic, Europe went into a frenzy. Other explorers and adventurers lined up for the chance to race to the Indies. Some wanted to follow Columbus's southerly route. But others, like John Cabot, felt that the fastest way to the Indies was a shorter, more northern passage.

John Cabot (1450–1499)

John Cabot was born in Genoa around 1451 as Giovanni Caboto. He may have known Christopher Columbus as a young boy, although no records prove they met. When he was about ten years old, Cabot moved with his family to Venice, Italy. At the time, Venice was a great trading center and seaport. Cabot learned the basics of navigation and became a seaman on a trading **galley** that traveled to ports in the Mediterranean Sea. As a young man in 1476, he took command of his own trading galley.

WORDS to KNOW

galley: a long ship with oars, used for war or trading.

Cabot studied navigational charts. Like Columbus, he was convinced that Asia could be reached more easily and quickly by sailing west through the Ocean Sea. Cabot reasoned that if Columbus had found the outlying islands of China, then the mainland must be farther north.

He asked the **monarchs** of both Portugal and Spain to sponsor his westward voyage to Asia. But the Portuguese king felt he had enough explorers to lead expeditions around the tip of Africa. In Spain, King Ferdinand and Queen Isabella had already agreed to sponsor Columbus.

WORDS *to* KNOW

monarch: a ruler such as a king or queen.

English merchants were at the end of the spice route. This meant they paid the highest prices for goods from the Indies.

Discouraged, Cabot moved to the English seaport of Bristol. Cabot correctly thought the English merchants would be interested in finding a shorter, more direct route to the Indies that would result in cheaper prices.

Wasting little time, Cabot traveled to London to meet with King Henry VII. Years before, the king had refused to sponsor Columbus, believing that his plan was unlikely to succeed. Now that Columbus had returned successfully from his first voyage, King Henry was eager to send his own expedition to find Asia. If John Cabot succeeded, it would bring huge riches to England.

DID YOU KNOW?

John Cabot's Italian last name, Caboto, means "coastal seaman."

SEARCHING FOR THE NORTHWEST PASSAGE

In 1496, King Henry VII issued letters to allow Cabot to sail in eastern, western, and northern seas that had not been explored by the Spanish or Portuguese. The king declared that any land Cabot found would belong to England, if Spain had not already claimed it.

After a failed first voyage due to bad weather, Cabot tried again, setting sail from Bristol on May 20, 1497. He sailed in one small ship, the *Mathew*, with a crew of about 18 men. After passing southern Ireland, Cabot turned west. He sailed along the route that the Vikings had used centuries before.

WORDS to KNOW

Northwest Passage: a sea route along the northern coast of North America, connecting the Atlantic and Pacific Oceans.

Northeast Passage: a sea route along the northern coast of Europe and Asia, connecting the Atlantic and Pacific oceans.

ice breaker: a ship that can break a channel through the ice.

The Northeast Passage

While some explorers tried to find the **Northwest Passage** to the Indies, others attempted to find the **Northeast Passage** above Europe and Russia. The English sponsored the first attempt in 1553. Holland, Denmark, and Sweden also sent explorers looking for the Northeast Passage. It was not until 1879 that Swedish explorer Nils Nordenskoild completed the first successful northeast voyage. The route he found became important for Russian ships. The waters are so cold that **ice breakers** have to be used to navigate these icy seas. ∾

WORDS *to* KNOW

foliage: the leaves of plants and trees.

inland: away from the sea.

After more than a month at sea, Cabot spotted land on June 24. He dropped anchor, rowed ashore, and planted the royal flag of England. Looking around, Cabot saw tall trees, rich grasses, and forests with beautiful **foliage**. Although he did not meet any native people, he saw signs that someone lived there. There was a site where a fire had been made, manure from farm animals, and a carved, painted stick pierced at both ends. Fearful of angry natives, Cabot decided not to travel with his small crew farther **inland**.

DID YOU KNOW?

A kind of fish called cod was plentiful in the waters Cabot explored. His crew could catch all they wanted by simply lowering baskets into the water.

Cabot then sailed along the coast for about 30 days before heading back to England. When he arrived on August 6, 1497, he gave the king glowing reports of what he had found. Although he was sure that he had landed on Asia, Cabot carried no gold or spices back to the king. But he did map the first details of the North American coast.

King Henry called Cabot's discovery "new-found land." It would eventually become known as Newfoundland, part of present-day Canada. The king was so pleased he gave Cabot a small reward and an annual pension for his service. Cabot spent that winter as a celebrity, dressed in rich silks. Wherever Cabot went, people followed him, hoping to meet him and shake his hand.

WORDS to KNOW

hull: the hollow, lowest part of a ship.

News spread all over Europe that Cabot had found Asia.

The next year, King Henry agreed to sponsor Cabot on a second voyage. Cabot set sail again from Bristol in May 1498 with five ships. Soon, however, he ran into heavy storms near Ireland and one ship was forced to sail back to port. The remaining four ships headed west across the Ocean Sea. John Cabot and his ships were never heard from again.

DID YOU KNOW?

Norwegian explorer Roald Amundsen discovered the Northwest Passage in 1903. Even though many explorers searched for it, few sailors use the Northwest Passage today because it is too stormy.

Cabot left behind little information about his expeditions. Except for his map, most of what historians know today has come from accounts by other people. Though he did not know it, John Cabot had discovered North America for the Europeans. His discovery would become more valuable than a ship's **hull** filled with treasure. It allowed England to claim North America.

A SAILOR'S DICE GAME

To pass the time on long sea voyages, sailors often played dice games. Try your hand at this version of a popular sixteenth-century game called liar's dice!

1 Divide the markers evenly among the players. To begin play, each player rolls one die. The highest roller goes first, and then play moves to the left.

2 The first player shakes the five dice in his cup, and then turns the cup upside down on the table, covering his dice. The player peeks at his dice, not letting the other players see what he has. The player may choose to keep his dice, or the player can roll any number of dice again. When he is finished, the player announces, or calls, his hand. But he does not show the other players the dice.

SUPPLIES

⅄ chips, pennies, or pebbles to use as markers

⅄ 5 dice per player

⅄ 1 cup per player to hide dice

3 The hands are ranked in this order: five of a kind, four of a kind, full house (three of a kind and one pair), high straight (2-3-4-5-6), low straight (1-2-3-4-5), two pair, and one pair.

4 When he is finished, the next player goes. He may call his hand if it is higher than the first player's. Note: players may "bluff" what they have under their cups. That is why the game is called "liar's dice"!

5 If someone does not believe a player's call, they can challenge them. If the challenger is wrong and the player was being honest, they put a chip or marker into the pot. If the player was bluffing, he must put a chip into the pot.

6 A new round begins after a challenge. The game is over when only one person has any markers remaining.

DID YOU KNOW?

Sailors often sang rhythmic work songs to help them with repetitive tasks such as hauling ropes.

CLASSROOM CONNECTION:

Organize a liar's dice tournament with your classmates. Who will win?

MAKE YOUR OWN
OCEAN IN A BOTTLE

You do not need to go to the beach to see ocean waves. Create your own at home!

1 Wash and dry a 2-liter plastic bottle and remove all labels. Fill the bottle halfway with tap water and add a few drops of blue food coloring. Swirl it around to mix. Then add glitter and sea creatures.

2 Using a funnel, fill the rest of the bottle with vegetable or mineral oil. Be sure that the rim and cap are dry, then apply white craft glue around the rim and seal the cap.

3 Use a layer of hot glue around the outer edge of the cap to seal against leakage.

4 Turn the bottle on its side and gently rock it to create your own ocean wave!

WHY IT WORKS: Oil is lighter than water, so the oil will float to the top and stay there. The two liquids will never mix, even when you tilt the bottle to create waves.

SUPPLIES

- empty 2-liter plastic bottle with cap
- water
- blue food coloring
- 1 teaspoon glitter
- small toy starfish, shells, and other sea creatures
- funnel
- clear vegetable oil or mineral oil
- white craft glue
- hot glue and glue gun

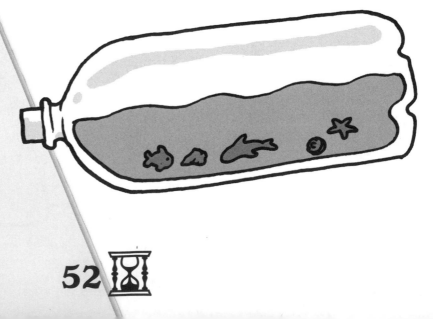

Chapter 4
Circling the Globe, Ferdinand Magellan

After Columbus discovered a westward route to what he thought was the Indies, the race heated up between Spain and Portugal to claim the Spice Islands. The Spice Islands were a group of tiny islands located between the Pacific and Indian Oceans. Valuable spices such as nutmeg and cloves grew on the islands. The country that controlled the islands and their spices would be rich and powerful.

WORDS *to* KNOW

astronomy:
the study of stars, planets, and space.

A young man from Portugal named Ferdinand Magellan was excited to hear about the discoveries of Columbus. Magellan served in the royal court of Portugal's King John II, and later King Manuel I. There he had learned **astronomy**, mapmaking, and navigation. He wanted to be part of the exciting world of the explorers.

When Magellan was 25 years old, King Manuel sent him to join a large fleet of ships guarding the east coast of Africa. The Portuguese didn't want anyone else using the sea route to the Indies.

Magellan sailed on many expeditions, visiting places like India, Africa, and the Spice Islands. He sailed farther east and discovered the Philippine Islands. He also proved his bravery in several battles for Portugal.

Ferdinand Magellan (1480–1521)

Magellan left the Portuguese court in 1516 after a disagreement with King Manuel. Around that time, people were slowly realizing that Columbus had not found the Indies, but instead had discovered a New World. Little was known about this New World. And no one had found a way to sail to the other side of the new continents.

Magellan thought that the Spice Islands must be close to the other side of the new continents. He also believed that he could find a western passage to the Spice Islands by following the South American coast. The new continent must eventually come to an end, just like Africa, and lead to the west.

WORDS *to* KNOW

humidity: moisture in the air.

Timekeeping

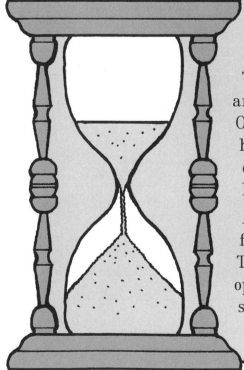

Sailors didn't have clocks, so they used a simple hourglass to measure the passage of time. It was made from two glass bottles, connected by a narrow tube. One of the glass bottles was filled with fine sand. When a sailor turned the hourglass upside down, the sand particles flowed from the top bottle, through the narrow neck, and into the bottom bottle. The sand flowed steadily and slowly, taking a certain amount of time to empty completely into the lower half. Once the upper half was empty, a sailor turned the hourglass again to begin measuring another period of time. During Magellan's voyage, each of his ships kept 18 hourglasses.

Although hourglasses were useful on voyages, many factors influenced how well they measured time. The **humidity** in the glass, or any change in the opening of the glass's neck, could affect how fast the sand flowed through the glass. This would result in an inaccurate measurement of time. ∾

WORDS *to* KNOW

strait: a narrow stretch of water that connects two larger bodies of water.

monopoly: complete control of something, like a service or product.

Magellan traveled to Spain and convinced King Charles I that he could find a **strait** through the New World to the Spice Islands. Magellan promised King Charles that he would claim the valuable islands for Spain. If he succeeded, Spain would be able to break Portugal's **monopoly** on a sea route to the Indies.

King Charles approved Magellan's plan and gave him money to prepare five ships. On September 20, 1519, Magellan and his ships set sail. He carried about 270 men, trinkets for trade, and enough food to last for two years.

Magellan had heard that a Portuguese fleet was waiting to stop him, so he didn't follow Columbus's route to the New World. Instead, he sailed down the west coast of Africa.

Like Columbus, Magellan was a foreigner in charge of a Spanish crew. The men did not trust him. They wanted to follow Columbus's proven route. Wary of Magellan's plans, several of his captains plotted mutiny to kill the commander. After a struggle, Magellan regained control of the crew. Magellan continued to sail his new route across the Atlantic.

DID YOU KNOW?

The five ships in Magellan's fleet were the *Trinidad, Concepción, San Antonio, Victoria*, and *Santiago*. Magellan sailed on the *Trinidad*.

On December 13, he reached Brazil at present-day Rio de Janeiro. There he traded trinkets with friendly natives for fresh food and water. Magellan then sailed down the east coast of South America. He tested every **cove** and river mouth for a route that crossed the continent to the other side. Unfortunately, the farther south Magellan's ships sailed, the colder the weather turned as winter began. The cold, empty waters upset the men. They wondered how much more Magellan would press south. They wanted to sail back across the Atlantic and reach the Spice Islands using a proven route.

WORDS *to* KNOW

cove: a small, sheltered **inlet** along a coast.

inlet: a narrow body of water that leads inland from a larger body of water.

Instead, Magellan ordered the fleet to drop anchor in Patagonia. This is in present-day Argentina. He decided they would settle there to wait out the winter. Many of the crew were not happy about Magellan's decision to stay. They grew even angrier when he refused to discuss it with them. Three of the ships rose in mutiny against Magellan. But with the help of those still loyal to him, Magellan was able to stop the rebellion.

Diseases on Board

Disease and sickness were often part of a sailor's voyage. Sailors were cold and wet much of the time. Limited food supplies often meant the men ate a poor diet. A disease called scurvy often affected sailors on long voyages. It was caused by a lack of vitamin C, found in fresh fruits and vegetables. Sailors with scurvy suffered from rotting skin and gums, which caused their teeth to fall out. If left untreated, scurvy results in death. ∿

With the mutiny over, Magellan and his crew settled down to wait for spring. They built huts, hunted seabirds, and gathered firewood. One ship had been lost when searching for winter quarters, but they repaired the four remaining ships. The cold days dragged on for six months. Finally, when the first signs of spring appeared, Magellan continued heading south. Now that the ships were close to the South Pole, each day was stormy, dark, and cold.

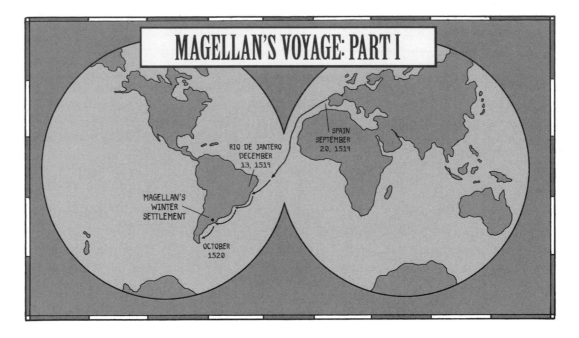

MAGELLAN'S VOYAGE: PART I

Finally, in October 1520, the fleet sighted a bay with black waters and snowcapped mountain peaks. The sailors believed it was not worth exploring. But Magellan would take no chances of missing his path through South America. He ordered two of his ships to sail into the bay as far as they could and return by the fifth day. Four days passed with no signs of the ships. Magellan was certain they had been lost in a fierce storm. But on the fifth day, the ships appeared in the bay with flags flying. Their crews jumped and waved from the decks. They had found a strait that seemed to lead west!

WORDS to KNOW

channel: a narrow stretch of water between two areas of land.

glaciers: huge sheets of ice found in mountains or polar regions.

provisions: supplies of food.

rations: the amount of food given for each meal.

galley: a ship's kitchen.

Spirits high, Magellan and his entire fleet sailed into the deep and narrow passage that is now called the Strait of Magellan. It was a dangerous place for sailing. The 344-mile **channel** (554 kilometers) ran through a twisted maze of reefs and islands. Ice-covered mountains and **glaciers** rose around them. Fierce winds tossed the ships. During the passage, the captain of the supply ship turned his ship around and headed back to Spain, taking most of the fleet's **provisions** with him.

Finally, after 38 nail-biting days, Magellan and his three remaining ships emerged at the strait's western end. It was a spectacular moment in Magellan's career. He had found the passage through the Americas to the Indies.

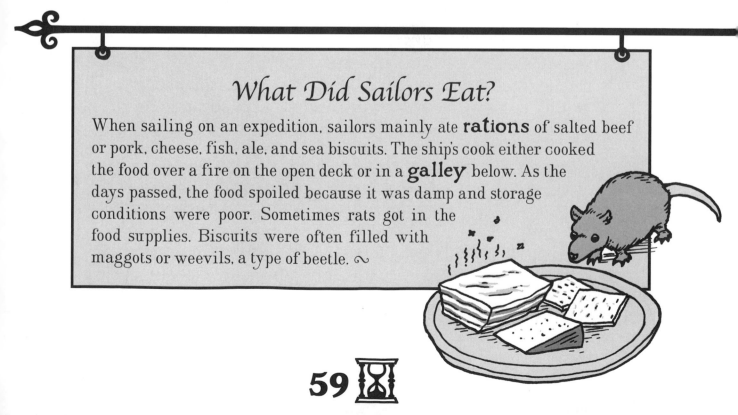

What Did Sailors Eat?

When sailing on an expedition, sailors mainly ate **rations** of salted beef or pork, cheese, fish, ale, and sea biscuits. The ship's cook either cooked the food over a fire on the open deck or in a **galley** below. As the days passed, the food spoiled because it was damp and storage conditions were poor. Sometimes rats got in the food supplies. Biscuits were often filled with maggots or weevils, a type of beetle. ∾

Patagonians (Big-Footed)

While Magellan was in Patagonia, a giant man who stood 7½ feet tall (2 meters) appeared. He danced and threw sand on his white hair. Magellan realized this was a sign of friendship. Soon other giant people appeared. Magellan called them Patagonians, which was Spanish for big-footed, because they wrapped their feet in animal skins stuffed with straw. ∽

Now Magellan faced an even greater challenge: the Pacific Ocean. It is the largest ocean on Earth, covering about one-third of the globe. Europeans knew little about it. An explorer named Balboa and a few traders in the Far East had seen it, but none suspected how wide it really was.

DID YOU KNOW?

The Pacific end of the Panama Canal is named after Vasco Nuñez de Balboa.

The new ocean was peaceful on the day Magellan entered it after crossing the harrowing waters of the strait, so he named it the Pacific. The word *Pacific* means peaceful.

He believed that the Spice Islands were only three days away. On November 28, 1520, Magellan's three remaining ships set sail on the unknown sea, headed for the Spice Islands.

Here Magellan made a great miscalculation. Instead of three days, the voyage took over three months. Day after day, the vast ocean surrounded them.

Conditions on the ships grew desperate. There was no fresh food or water. Their sea biscuits crawled with worms and maggots. As food ran out, the crew began to starve. Even the water turned **putrid** and yellow with **bacteria**. The men were forced to eat rats, sawdust, and leather barrel straps to survive. Most became sick with scurvy. Their arms and legs swelled. Their gums turned blue and their teeth fell out. Twenty-nine men died and the situation looked grim.

WORDS *to* KNOW

putrid: decaying and smelling bad.

bacteria: very tiny living things that decay food and can be harmful.

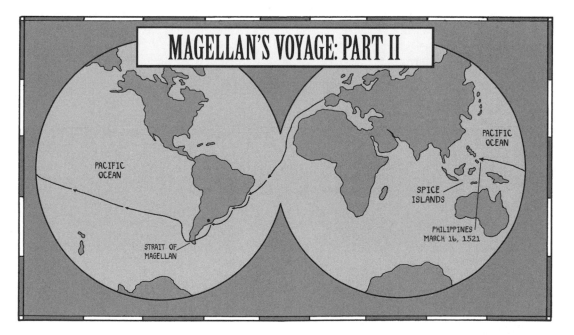

MAGELLAN'S VOYAGE: PART II

PACIFIC OCEAN

PACIFIC OCEAN

SPICE ISLANDS

PHILIPPINES MARCH 16, 1521

STRAIT OF MAGELLAN

Then on March 6, 1521, the loud call of "Land!" rang out over the ships. Relieved, Magellan and the men joyously celebrated. They believed that they had finally reached the Spice Islands. Actually, it was the island of Guam. Still, the people of Guam were friendly and the crew loaded the ships with badly needed fresh fruit, vegetables, meat, and water.

WORDS *to* KNOW

circumnavigate: to go all the way around.

After nine days on Guam, Magellan sailed again to the Philippines. His March 16 arrival was a moment of triumph for Magellan. He had reached these islands before by sailing east around Africa. Putting the two voyages together, he was the first man to **circumnavigate** the globe.

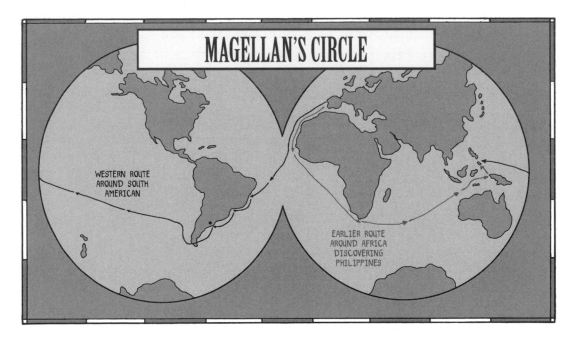

MAGELLAN'S CIRCLE

WESTERN ROUTE AROUND SOUTH AMERICAN

EARLIER ROUTE AROUND AFRICA DISCOVERING PHILIPPINES

Magellan claimed the Philippine Islands for Spain. He also wanted to convert the native people to Christianity. On the islands of Cebu and Mazzava, Magellan's conversion ceremonies went well. However, the chief on Cebu told Magellan about a small island called Mactan where the chief refused to convert to Christianity. Against the advice of many, Magellan decided to take Mactan by force. He believed a group of natives was no match for his experienced, well-armed Spanish men. He also felt an impressive show of Spanish force would keep the remaining local tribes loyal to Spain after he left.

DID YOU KNOW?

King Charles sold Spain's claim to the Spice Islands to Portugal for 350,000 ducats in 1529. This wold be tens of millions of dollars today.

On April 26, Magellan attacked Mactan. But Magellan forgot about the reefs along the beaches. His ships could not get close enough to fire their cannons. With about 60 armed men, Magellan rowed ashore. They were met by more than 1,500 natives charging them, whooping and yelling. The Spanish fired their guns and crossbows. In return, the natives shot arrows and hurled bamboo spears at the Spaniards.

How Fast?

Sailors during the 1500s did not have speedometers to tell them how fast they were going. Instead, they used a rope with evenly spaced knots tied into it. Then they tied the rope to a wooden log and tossed the log off the back of the ship. The rope was let out so the log stayed in the same place in the water. Sailors could estimate how fast they were going by counting how many knots they let out in 30 seconds. This is how knots became the measure of a ship's speed. Today, one knot is equal to one nautical mile (6,076 feet or 1,852 meters) per hour. ∾

Magellan was shot through the right leg with a poisoned arrow. A native hurled a spear into his face and another wounded him in the arm. Magellan fell into the water and the natives rushed forward to stab him to death. The remaining sailors retreated as fast as they could and sailed away.

DID YOU KNOW?

We have details of Magellan's expedition because Antonio Pigafetta, a survivor, recorded the entire journey in a diary.

With Magellan dead, Sebastian del Cano took command of the fleet. He decided to sail for the Spice Islands where they could fill their ships with riches. Because the remaining 115 men were not enough to sail three ships, del Cano ordered the men to burn one ship. Without Magellan to lead them, the men struggled for six months to reach the Spice Islands. They finally arrived in November and the greedy sailors loaded the ships with spices, silks, gold, and gems.

WORDS *to* KNOW

evade: to keep away or avoid.

To make sure that at least one ship survived the return trip to Spain, del Cano ordered that they take different routes.

One ship was seized by the Portuguese, who took the cargo and killed most of her crew. The other ship, however, managed to **evade** Portuguese ships as it crossed the Indian Ocean and rounded Africa's Cape of Good Hope. On September 6, 1522, the last ship of Magellan's fleet, the *Victoria*, sailed into a Spanish harbor with just 18 survivors. It had taken almost three years, but it was the first ship to sail around the world.

The passage that Magellan worked so hard to discover would never be used as a regular trade route. But he had discovered something far more important. Magellan's voyage showed Europeans how big the world really was. Before his trip, they believed that the world was mostly land. Now they knew that two-thirds of it was actually water.

The exploration of the world's oceans had begun with Prince Henry the Navigator. Now the process of discovery would turn inland, as explorers searched for the secrets inside the New World.

WORDS *to* KNOW

dysentery: an infection of the intestines.

Sir Francis Drake

After Magellan proved it was possible to sail around the world, other explorers followed in his footsteps. In 1577, England's Queen Elizabeth I gave Sir Francis Drake five ships and sent him on an expedition around the world to find treasure and spices.

Like Magellan, Drake did not have an easy journey. He lost two ships off the coast of South America. Two others were lost in the Strait of Magellan. He and his crew weathered storms, illness, food shortages, and threats of mutiny.

After passing through the Strait of Magellan, Drake sailed north, landing off the coast of present-day California. He then travelled up to what would later become the United States–Canada border. Crossing the Pacific and Indian Oceans, he navigated around the tip of Africa and finally landed back in England in 1580 with a ship full of treasure. He had completed the second voyage around the world. Pleased with his success, the queen made Drake a knight and gave him a reward of 10,000 pounds, which was a large amount of money at the time. In 1596, Drake died near Panama from **dysentery**. ∾

MAKE YOUR OWN
SAND HOURGLASS

Sailors used a simple hourglass to measure the passage of time. In this project you will create your own hourglass just like the ones the explorers used to tell time on ships.

1 Because this project can get messy, you may want to do it outside, or cover your workspace with newspaper.

2 Take a clean, dry, plastic soda bottle, and place your funnel in the bottle's opening. Pour sand into the funnel until the bottle is about three-quarters full.

3 Place a small square of aluminum foil over the opening of the sand-filled bottle. Poke a hole in the center of the foil using a sharpened pencil.

4 Turn the empty bottle upside down and tape its opening to the opening of the first bottle. Do not use too much tape yet because you may need to redo it.

5 Flip your plastic bottle hourglass over so that the empty one is now on bottom. Use a stopwatch to time how long it takes for the sand to completely empty into the bottom bottle. If you want a 2-minute timer, adjust the sand and try it again. Once you have the right amount of sand, tape the bottles securely with duct tape.

SUPPLIES

- Y 2 two-liter plastic soda bottles
- Y funnel
- Y bucket of sand
- Y aluminum foil
- Y sharpened pencil
- Y duct tape
- Y stopwatch

DID YOU KNOW?

Celestial navigation was a way of judging where a ship was, based on the sun or stars above.

MAKE YOUR OWN SEA BISCUITS

Sea biscuits were a common food for sailors on long journeys across the ocean because they could last for years if kept dry. Make your own sea biscuits and see what you think! You will be using a hot oven, so be sure to have an adult help you with this project.

1 Preheat your oven to 325 degrees Fahrenheit (165 degrees Celsius). Mix flour, water, and salt in a mixing bowl until a dough forms.

2 Roll the dough on a floured surface until it is about a half-inch thick.

3 Cut the dough into 3-inch-wide pieces. Place on a baking sheet and poke holes in each with a fork.

4 Bake the biscuits until they are slightly browned. The baked biscuits will be hard! Sailors softened their biscuits in liquids like coffee, stew, soup, or water.

SUPPLIES

- Y oven
- Y 2 cups flour
- Y $\frac{1}{2}$ cup water
- Y salt to taste
- Y mixing bowl
- Y wooden spoon
- Y rolling pin
- Y floured surface
- Y knife
- Y baking sheet
- Y fork

DID YOU KNOW?

Before eating their biscuits, sailors would tap them on the table to knock out small beetles. Or they would put them in their soup and wait for the maggots to float to the top. Then they could scoop them out.

MAKE YOUR OWN
SAILOR'S LANYARD

During their free time on long sea journeys, sailors tied knots and made items such as lanyards from rope and knots. A lanyard is used to secure or hang a small object such as a whistle or a key, and is usually worn around the neck or wrist.

SUPPLIES

ϒ 2 plastic laces in different colors, each about 24 inches long

ϒ key ring

ϒ scissors

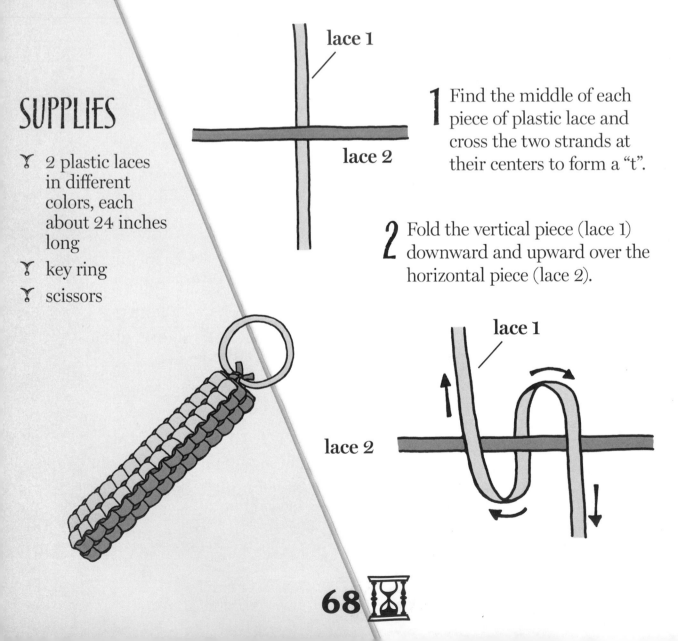

lace 1

lace 2

1 Find the middle of each piece of plastic lace and cross the two strands at their centers to form a "t".

2 Fold the vertical piece (lace 1) downward and upward over the horizontal piece (lace 2).

lace 1

lace 2

3 Fold the right piece of lace 2 to the left. Weave the end of lace 2 over the nearest strand of lace 1 and under the farthest strand of lace 1.

4 Repeat step 3 in reverse by folding the left piece of lace 2 to the right over the nearest strand of lace 1 and weaving it under the farthest strand of lace 1.

5 Pull all four ends of lace tight and your knot should have a square box shape.

6 Turn your knot back over. Make another box knot by folding the top piece of lace 1 down and the bottom piece of lace 1 up. Weave the left side of lace 2 over, then under, the strands of lace 1. Repeat with the right side of lace 2. Pull tight.

7 Repeat this box knot process until your lanyard is a long as you want it. Tie a knot to finish it off.

8 Insert the key ring through the knot and tie a second knot around the key ring, securing it to the lanyard. Trim any long pieces to the desired length.

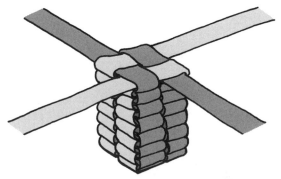

MAKE YOUR OWN
PAPIER MACHE GLOBE

Cover your workspace with newspaper before you begin.

1 Rip newspaper into small strips, about 1 inch by 3 inches ($2\frac{1}{2}$ by $7\frac{1}{2}$ centimeters), and set aside.

2 In a bowl, mix equal parts of white school glue and warm water. Soak your newspaper strips in this mixture for a few minutes.

3 Blow up the balloon and carefully cover it with the soaked newspaper strips. After you completely cover the balloon, let it dry fully for about a day. Repeat the process until you have three layers of newspaper on your balloon, making sure you let the balloon dry in between each layer.

4 After the final layer has dried, use a pencil or marker to mark the North and South Poles on your globe. Draw a ring around the globe to represent the equator. Then draw the seven continents onto your globe. Use the map of the world to guide you.

5 Paint the continents green and the remaining areas blue. When all the paint has dried, use a black permanent marker to add details and labels to your globe.

SUPPLIES

Y newspaper
Y bowl
Y white school glue
Y water
Y round balloon
Y pencil or marker
Y map of the world
Y paint: brown, blue, green
Y paintbrush
Y black permanent marker
Y yarn: 3 different colors each 18 inches long (45 centimeters)

CLASSROOM CONNECTION:
Use the three different colors of yarn to map the routes of men such as Columbus, Magellan, and Cabot. Glue the yarn along the routes.

MAKE YOUR OWN
COCONUT MILK

People in the Philippines, where Magellan stopped, often drank fresh coconut milk. Now you can make your own!

1 Have an adult help you pierce the eyes of a fresh coconut with an ice pick and drain the juice inside. Set the juice aside.

2 Bake the coconut in the oven at 325 degrees Fahrenheit (165 degrees Celsius) for about 30 minutes.

3 Remove the coconut from the oven and let it cool a bit. Then have an adult help you crack it with a hammer so that the shell breaks into several pieces.

4 Remove all the coconut meat from the shell. Then peel off the brown skin and cut the meat into very small cubes.

5 Place the white pieces of coconut meat in the food processor. Add the coconut juice and enough water to cover the coconut meat. Blend at high speed until completely mixed.

6 Strain the liquid and take a taste of your coconut milk! Any leftovers can be refrigerated for 1 to 2 days.

SUPPLIES

- coconut
- ice pick
- oven
- hammer
- knife
- food processor
- water
- strainer
- glass

Chapter Five

The Spanish Conquistadors

By the 1500s, amazing stories about gold in the New World had spread throughout Europe. Some tales told of a city made of gold, which the Spanish called El Dorado. While Portugal led the search for a sea route to the Indies in the 1400s, Spanish explorers took the lead to explore the New World in the 1500s.

King Ferdinand and Queen Isabella wanted to claim the New World for Spain. It wasn't just about land and gold. Queen Isabella also wanted to spread Christianity to more people. With support from the king and queen, Spanish explorers sailed to the New World. These men were called **conquistadors**, which means conqueror in Spanish. They traveled to find gold, claim land, and to spread Christianity.

In fact, priests often traveled with the Conquistadors to help convert the native people to Christianity. Successful conquistadors were rewarded with money, land, and slaves.

So who were these Spanish conquistadors? Many were **nobles** who had education and a title, but little family wealth. Many came from Spain's military. These men faced countless dangers sailing across unmapped oceans and exploring new worlds for fame and fortune. The Conquistadors endured disease, starvation, and war. But finding gold meant a huge payoff.

WORDS *to* KNOW

noble: a person of high rank or birth.
land grant: a gift of land.

Hernán Cortés (1485–1547)

Hernán Cortés

Perhaps the greatest conquistador was Hernán Cortés, who was only seven years old when Christopher Columbus reached the New World. Cortés' father was a noble, but was not wealthy. Cortés knew that he would have to make his own fame and fortune.

For a while, Cortés studied law at the University of Salamanca. But he was hungry for adventure, so he left school and sailed to the New World in 1504. He received a **land grant** and settled down to farm on the island of Hispaniola. A few years later, Cortés helped Hispaniola's Spanish governor, Diego Velázquez, conquer Cuba. Cortés was rewarded with a larger land grant and several native slaves.

In 1517, explorers returning from Mexico's Yucatán peninsula told amazing stories of a rich civilization. The people there called themselves Mayans. Governor Velázquez decided to send an expedition to the Yucatan peninsula to find out for himself. He chose Cortés to lead the men.

To prepare for the journey, Cortés recruited about 100 sailors and more than 500 soldiers. He also had a doctor, several carpenters, a few hundred Cuban servants, some African slaves, a handful of women, and 16 horses. He loaded cannons, muskets, crossbows, and ammunition onto the ships and prepared to leave.

Governor Velázquez worried that Cortés's expedition was becoming much larger than he had intended. The governor sent orders for Cortés to step down as commander. But Cortés's brother-in-law intercepted the messenger and killed him. Cortés left before the governor could try to stop him again. As the sun rose on February 18, 1519, Cortés set sail for Mexico.

On the Yucatán coast, Cortés discovered a large Mayan settlement. The Mayans asked him to leave and a battle broke out. The Spanish won easily and the Mayan leaders pledged to obey Cortés.

The Mayans told Cortés about a rich and mighty kingdom farther inland. It was called the **Aztec** Empire and was ruled by Montezuma II. Eager to claim the Aztec treasures, Cortés marched his forces inland toward the Aztec capital city of Tenochtitlan.

Aztec Empire

When the Conquistadors arrived in the New World in the 1500s, the Aztecs ruled Mexico. Their capital city, Tenochtitlan, was on an island in the middle of a large lake. It was **prosperous**, clean, and bigger than any city in Spain. In 1519, more than 300,000 people lived in Tenochtitlan. They worked as merchants, farmers, and fishermen. Known as fierce warriors, the Aztecs battled neighboring villages to capture people. The lucky ones were **integrated** into Aztec society.

The Aztecs built many beautiful temples in the shape of pyramids, with four sides that were wider at the bottom. Stairs on one side led to the flat top, where religious **ceremonies** took place. The Great Pyramid of Tenochtitlan is one of the most well known of the Aztec temples. It was also called the Sun Pyramid. This temple may have been as tall as 200 feet when the Spanish arrived and painted a bright red, but it was almost completely destroyed by them. ∿

WORDS *to* KNOW

Aztecs: Mexican native people who built a great civilization before the conquest of Mexico by Cortés.

prosperous: wealthy.

integrate: to become part of.

ceremony: an event to celebrate or honor something, such as a god or a holiday.

WORDS *to* KNOW

alliance: a partnership between peoples or countries.

terrain: ground or land.

litter: a stretcher used to carry someone.

massacre: brutal killing of a large number of people.

Along the way, Cortés made **alliances** with native tribes who were enemies of the Aztecs. The Tlaxcalan tribe offered Cortés 10,000 warriors! For three months, the growing force traveled over 400 miles, across difficult **terrain**.

In November 1519, Cortés and his large army finally reached Tenochtitlan. As they drew near the city, crowds gathered to stare at the Spaniards and their horses. At the city's entrance, Montezuma arrived to meet Cortés, carried by his lords on a **litter** draped with fine cotton bedding. The Aztec leader welcomed Cortés to the city. The two men exchanged gifts of necklaces. The Aztecs then provided lodging for the Spanish in a beautiful palace.

DID YOU KNOW?

Aztec legend stated that their god, Quetzalcoatl, would return to Earth in the form of a light-skinned, bearded man to reclaim his rule over the Aztec people. Many believed that Cortés was Quetzalcoatl and welcomed him with gifts.

Cortés and his men were impressed with the treasures of the beautiful city.

Cortés grew uneasy. He knew that Montezuma's Aztecs greatly outnumbered his men. What were Montezuma's plans? Cortés decided not to wait to find out— he took Montezuma prisoner. With their leader held hostage, the Aztecs stood by as Spanish soldiers took over the city. Spanish priests began to remove images of the Aztec religion and replace them with Christian images.

Meanwhile, Governor Velázquez sent an army into Mexico to arrest Cortés. Cortés was forced to leave the Aztec capital to defend himself. With about 100 men, Cortés defeated Velázquez's force.

While he was gone, some of the Spanish in Tenochtitlan attacked an unarmed group of Aztecs during a religious festival.

The **massacre** stirred the Aztec people into an uprising. They cut off food supplies and attacked the palace where Cortés' men were staying.

When Cortés heard about the uprising, he quickly returned to Tenochtitlan. By the time he arrived, the situation had gotten worse. Cortés made Montezuma stand on the palace roof and try to calm the angry Aztec people. The people, however, were tired of the Spanish, their demands for gold, and their attacks on the Aztec religion. They threw stones and arrows at Montezuma, injuring him. It was clear that the great Aztec ruler no longer controlled his people. He died a few days later.

Desperate, Cortés and his men tried to escape the city on June 30, 1520. They took all the gold they could carry from the king's treasure house. It was a dark and rainy night, and during the retreat, the Aztecs attacked. In the confusion, hundreds of Spaniards fell into a canal and died, probably weighed down by the gold they carried. Several thousand Tlaxcalan allies were lost as well.

The night was so horrific it was called the Noche Triste or the "night of sorrows".

Cortés and his remaining men fled over the mountains to Tlaxcala. There he gathered more troops and supplies from Cuba. He recruited more native allies. In 1521, Cortés launched a new attack on Tenochtitlan with a force of more than 16,000 men. The new Aztec leader, Cuauhtémoc, prepared for the attack by building **barricades** and removing bridges from the **causeways**. But the Spanish had a new weapon. They did not realize it, but they had brought a new disease with them to the New World. An outbreak of **smallpox** weakened the Aztec defenders.

WORDS *to* KNOW

barricade: a barrier to stop people from getting past a certain point.

causeway: a raised road built across water or low ground.

smallpox: a deadly disease.

siege: surrounding a place, such as a city, to cut off supplies. It forces those inside to eventually surrender.

revenue: income or money.

DID YOU KNOW?

Montezuma asked Cortés what it would take to make the Spanish leave his empire. Cortés said, "We Spanish suffer from a disease of the heart, which can be cured only by gold."

For three months, Cortés fought to reach the center of Tenochtitlan. The fighting was so fierce that the waters around the city turned red with blood. When the **siege** was finally over, more than half a million Aztecs and native allies of Cortés had died. In addition to those killed in battle, many died from illness, starvation, or polluted water.

DID YOU KNOW?

Spanish colonists started a system called *encomienda*. Under this system, the natives were forced to give tribute to the Spanish. Tribute could be gold, or work by the native people. It often led to the natives being treated as slaves.

When the Aztecs surrendered, there were only about 30,000 people remaining in the once-proud city of 300,000.

New Spain

Cortés claimed the Aztec land for Spain. He loaded ships with Aztec treasures and sent them to Spain. After destroying the Aztec city, he built a new Spanish capital on the site. Mexico City soon became an important city in the Spanish colony of New Spain. New Spain was a huge source of **revenue** for the Spanish Empire.

Back in Spain, Cortés was a hero. The king forgave Cortés for his rebellion against Governor Velázquez. He made Cortés the governor and captain general of New Spain in 1523. Cortés would lead several more expeditions before returning to Spain, where he died of dysentery in 1547.

Ponce de León

WORDS *to* KNOW

province: a district or region of some countries.

Like many of the Conquistadors, Ponce de León trained as a soldier in the Spanish military. He joined Christopher Columbus on his second voyage to the New World in 1493 and settled on Hispaniola, where he became the governor of a **province**.

In 1506, Ponce de León discovered a nearby island that he named Puerto Rico. He was the island's governor until 1511, when the king replaced him with Columbus's son.

Ponce de León had heard stories about an island to the north that was full of rich treasure. The island was also supposed to have a magical spring whose waters could make old people young again.

In 1513, de León sailed north and landed on Florida's east coast, near present-day St. Augustine. He claimed the land for Spain and named it La Florida or place of flowers. He sailed down the east coast, up the west coast, and through the Florida Keys. Eventually, de León turned his ships back to Puerto Rico.

In 1521, de León returned to Florida to build a colony. He landed with 200 men on the west coast. Native American warriors met the Spanish and a fight broke out. Their arrows wounded Ponce de León and many of his men. The Spanish decided to abandon their colony. Ponce de León would eventually die from his wound in Cuba in July 1521.

Ponce de León (1460–1521)

Francisco Pizarro

While Cortés was conquering the Aztecs in Mexico, another conquistador mounted an attack against the mighty Incas in Peru. Francisco Pizarro was born in Spain in 1475. With little chance of wealth or titles from his family, Pizarro joined the military. As a soldier, he traveled around Europe and gained valuable experience.

Pizarro first traveled to the New World in 1502 on an expedition to Hispaniola. Once in the New World, Pizarro explored Panama and Columbia. In 1513, he joined Balboa's expedition that discovered the Pacific Ocean.

In Panama, Pizarro set up a new Spanish colony, where he grew wealthy as a farmer and part owner of a gold mine.

Francisco Pizarro (1478–1541)

While in Panama, Pizarro heard stories about a rich native empire to the south. Eager to claim new riches, he planned a voyage down the coast of South America with a partner named Diego de Almagro. Their first attempt failed, but they tried again in 1526. They gathered together 160 men, two ships, and several horses and headed south.

WORDS to KNOW

balsa: a very light wood.

After setting up camp near the San Juan River in present-day Columbia, Pizarro sent half the forces ahead as scouts. While near present-day Ecuador, the scouts met several Incas on a **balsa** trading raft. To their delight, the Spanish discovered that the raft contained treasures such as silver, gold, precious stones, and woven fabrics. With sign language, the Incas said that their gold had come from a land far to the south.

Meanwhile, the men camping with Pizarro grew restless. Starving and sick, they sent messages back to Panama asking to be rescued from Pizarro. Furious, Pizarro drew a line in the sand. He told the men that if any wished to continue with him, they should step over the line. Thirteen men took the challenge and stepped over the line.

Pizarro and his 13 men continued sailing south. They landed at the Inca city of Tumbes, in present-day Peru. They could barely contain their excitement as they traveled farther south and met more friendly natives with valuable objects.

The Spanish were amazed to see many gold
and silver objects and decorations.

Certain that he had found the rich Inca civilization, Pizarro returned to Panama. He was not satisfied to explore and trade with the Incas. Instead, Pizarro planned to conquer the native Inca people. He wanted to claim their land and treasures for Spain. Pizarro traveled to Spain and presented the Spanish King Charles V with golden treasures from the Incas. The king and queen agreed to support Pizarro on his quest to conquer Peru. They also made him governor of Peru.

Pizarro returned to the New World with 200 men and 3 ships. In 1531, his third expedition left Panama. Instead of traveling by sea, Pizarro marched his men by land down the coast to Tumbes.

DID YOU KNOW?

Many of the old Inca traditions, festivals, and pilgrimages survived in secret, or were combined with Christian ones.

Killer Diseases

European explorers brought new diseases with them to the New World. The immune systems of Europeans had built up some resistance to these diseases over the centuries, but the native population had no **immunity** whatsoever. Smallpox, measles, bubonic plague, and influenza swept through the native population. These diseases killed large numbers of people and played a big role in the downfall of native civilizations. ∾

WORDS to KNOW

immunity: able to resist a disease.

He found Tumbes in ruins. While Pizarro was gone, the two sons of the Incan emperor had fought in a bloody civil war. The son named Atahualpa had won the war. The other son, Huáscar, was now a prisoner, but he still had many loyal supporters throughout the empire.

Pizarro decided to use the civil war to his advantage. First he made alliances with natives who were still loyal to Huáscar. Then he marched his forces to meet Atahualpa. Pizarro told Atahualpa that they intended to take over the land and convert everyone to Christianity. When a fight erupted, Pizarro ordered his men to attack.

Spanish soldiers fired their guns into the crowd, killing about 10,000 Incas. Only five Spanish died.

The victorious Pizarro founded a capital city in 1535 that is known today as Lima. But Pizarro faced threats from his own side. His partner Almagro grew unhappy with his share of the Inca treasure. He and his supporters attacked Pizarro's forces. When Almagro was defeated, he was publicly beheaded for his betrayal. Almagro's family and followers captured Pizarro in his palace in Lima. In revenge, they assassinated Pizarro in 1541.

WORDS *to* **KNOW**

loot: to steal money or treasure.

Pizarro's expeditions had a lasting impact on the history and culture of modern Peru. After Pizarro conquered the Inca people, more Spaniards moved to Peru. They **looted** Inca treasures and sent them to Europe. The Spanish also destroyed Inca temples and towns and replaced them with Spanish churches and cities. Many native Incas died from new diseases. The Spanish forced the rest to adopt Spanish clothing and food, and to convert to Christianity.

Hernando de Soto (1500–1542)

Hernando de Soto

Hernando de Soto was a conquistador who traveled with Pizarro's army to Peru in 1532. In 1538, the king appointed de Soto the governor of Cuba. As governor, de Soto had the right to conquer and colonize the territory north of Cuba. It was a vast, unexplored region that was supposed to be rich in gold and silver. Ponce de Leon had visited the land a few years earlier in 1513, but much was still unknown.

Tempted by the promise of great wealth, de Soto gathered a large, well-equipped force to explore and conquer North America.

DID YOU KNOW?

Hernando de Soto was the first European to see the Mississippi River.

In May 1539, he sailed with a fleet of nine ships to Florida's west coast. De Soto landed at present-day Tampa Bay. He marched his men and horses north from Florida, then west towards the Mississippi River. Along the way, they discovered many native people and stores of corn, but no gold.

De Soto quickly became known as a cruel and bloody leader. Desperate for gold, de Soto ordered his men to capture and torture natives to make them tell him where the gold was located. After torturing the captives, the Spanish often killed them. De Soto's men also stole anything of value from the natives, sometimes even robbing graves.

De Soto's expedition reached the Mississippi River near present-day Memphis, Tennessee. They crossed the river in boats, and then traveled northwest through Arkansas. On their return in the spring, de Soto fell ill with a fever. By June 1542, de Soto was dead. His men placed his body in a dug-out tree trunk and sank it in the Mississippi River.

De Soto never found gold, but his expedition was the first detailed exploration of the southeastern United States. He opened the west for future Spanish explorers. But de Soto is best remembered for the violence and death he brought upon the natives he met.

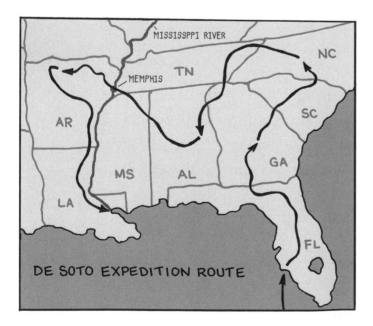

DE SOTO EXPEDITION ROUTE

Francisco de Coronado

Meanwhile, on the other side of the continent, Francisco de Coronado was also excited by the idea of great riches in North America. Coronado was a governor in Mexico when he heard about the legendary Seven Cities of Cibola, which were said to be filled with gold, silver, and jewels.

In February 1540, he led an expedition into what is now the southwestern United States. Traveling through New Mexico, Coronado was disappointed to discover that the fabled Seven Cities of Cibola were just the pueblos of the local Zuni tribe.

But Coronado heard about another city of great wealth to the east. Once again he was disappointed to find another poor tribe of natives. Although he never found the gold for which he searched, Coronado conquered several native villages. In addition, Coronado's men glimpsed one of North America's greatest treasures, the Grand Canyon.

Francisco de Coronado (1510–1554)

The Spanish conquistadors, like Cortés, Pizarro, de Soto, and Coronado, brought great wealth and power to Spain.

The new discoveries made by these explorers gave Spain the leading claim on land in the New World in the 1500s. Seeing Spain's growing power and revenue from the New World, other European countries were determined to send their own expeditions.

MAKE YOUR OWN
SPANISH GALLEON

A galleon was a large ship with many decks. It was used from the sixteenth through the eighteenth centuries. The Spanish transported a variety of goods from America to Spain in galleons.

1 Place one milk carton on its side. Cover the bottom half of the carton with black construction paper, using tape to secure. Bring the construction paper up along the back of the carton, leaving about 1 inch ($2\frac{1}{2}$ centimeters) to stick up over the top of the carton.

2 Tape white construction paper over the rest of the carton. Glue two mounds of play dough in the center of the carton.

3 Cut a 2-to-3-inch piece (5 to $7\frac{1}{2}$ centimeters) from the bottom of the second milk carton. Cover this piece with white construction paper. Place it over the play dough mounds and tape it to the first carton. Use a pencil to poke two holes in the second carton above the play dough mounds. Slide two straws through the holes in the second carton into the play dough.

4 Cut three white sails of different sizes from construction paper. Use markers or crayons to draw a red cross on the sails.

SUPPLIES

- Y 2 milk cartons
- Y black, white, and red construction paper
- Y scissors
- Y tape
- Y glue
- Y play dough
- Y pencil
- Y 2 straws
- Y hole punch
- Y markers or crayons

5 Use a hole punch to punch a hole in the top and bottom of each sail. Thread the sails onto the straw masts. The largest should go in the front, while the smaller two share a mast in the back.

6 Cut out a flag from red construction paper and tape it to the top of the first mast. Use markers to draw windows and doors on your ship.

CLASSROOM CONNECTION:

Using your galleon, identify five parts of a ship. Find the mast, hull, bow (front), stern (rear), and sail.

MAKE YOUR OWN BALSA RAFT

Early European explorers on the western coast of South America reported that native people made long sea voyages for trade. They used rafts made from logs of balsa wood lashed together. Spanish conquistadors noted that these rafts had cotton sails, like their own ships.

1 Lay 5 pieces of balsa wood next to each other. Glue them together to form a rectangular raft shape. Repeat with 5 more pieces of wood.

2 Place the two rafts end to end and glue them together to create one long raft.

3 Reinforce the joint between the two rafts by gluing a thin strip of balsa wood crosswise across the joint. Repeat on the underside of the raft. Let dry.

SUPPLIES

- Y 10 pieces of balsa wood, approximately 5 by ¾ inches (13 by 2 centimeters)
- Y glue
- Y 2 thin strips of balsa wood
- Y scissors
- Y white paper
- Y 2 wooden dowels, approximately 6 inches long (15 centimeters)
- Y 2 wooden dowels, about 8 inches long (20 centimeters)
- Y tape

4 Cut two triangular sails from a piece of white paper. Glue one of the shorter wooden dowels to the long side of each triangle. Let dry.

5 Push one longer wooden dowel into the center log on one side of your raft. Glue in place to form a mast. Repeat with the second longer dowel on the other side of your raft.

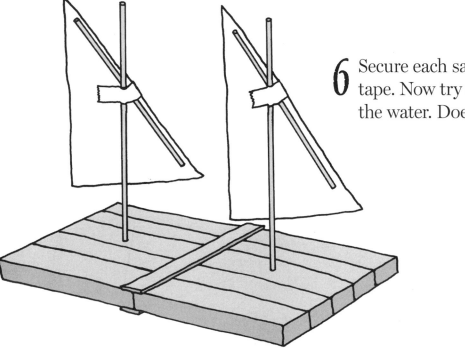

6 Secure each sail to a mast with tape. Now try out your raft in the water. Does it float?

MAKE YOUR OWN
SAILOR'S KNOT

Sailors used many different kinds of knots. The Sailor's Knot was used to tie two ropes together to secure a boat rope to another boat or to a dock.

SUPPLIES

⚲ 2 pieces of rope

1 Place your two ropes on a table or the floor facing each other. Make a loop with the right rope by passing the tail under its standing end.

STEP 1

2 Pass the left rope's end under the loop of the right rope and then over the standing end of the right rope, and under the tail.

STEP 2

3 Bring the left rope's end down into the loop of the right rope and weave it under its own standing end.

STEP 3

4 Pull both standing ends away from each other to tighten the knot.

STEP 4

Sometimes, sailors tied knots for fun, just to pass the time on long sea voyages! The figure-eight knot is a favorite because it is easy to tie and untie. It is also used to make grips on a climbing rope or to stop the end of a rope from pulling free.

1 Make a loop with one piece of rope.

2 Pass the working end behind the standing part of the rope.

3 Bring the end through the first loop to make an "eight" shape.

4 Tighten the knot by pulling on both ends.

STEP 1

STEP 2

STEP 3

STEP 4

CLASSROOM CONNECTION:

Using your sand hourglass from another activity, see how many knots you can tie before the sand runs out. Compare your results with your classmates.

MAKE YOUR OWN
AZTEC ART

Aztec art was used as a way to honor their gods and for communication. Stories were commonly written in pictures. Because the Aztec people had a strong appreciation for nature, their art often included a wide variety of insects, birds, fish, and animals. Jaguars, ducks, monkeys, snakes, deer, and dogs were common themes.

The animals represented gods and goddesses. The sun was also a common image in the center of Aztec art. Aztec pottery usually had geometric designs around the edge, like a zig-zag or squares.

SUPPLIES

- paper
- pencil
- internet access
- clay
- craft knife
- toothpicks

1 On a piece of paper, sketch a design for your Aztec art. You may want to look on the Internet for examples of Aztec symbols for inspiration.

2 Using the clay, make a round tablet. Carve designs around the edge with the craft knife.

3 Use toothpicks to carve Aztec symbols into your tablet. You may also choose to add symbols that represent important aspects of your own life.

Chapter 6

Journeys Inland

While the Spanish conquistadors searched for gold in the south, other Europeans sailed to the northern coasts of the New World. Some looked for the Northwest Passage they thought would lead to the riches of the Indies. Others explored to claim the vast resources of the New World.

NEW WORLD EXPLORATION
- ▨ AREAS EXPLORED BY SPAIN
- ☐ AREAS EXPLORED BY OTHER EUROPEAN NATIONS

Jacques Cartier

Jacques Cartier was born in Saint-Malo, an island off the north coast of France. His father was a fisherman and young Cartier often joined him on fishing trips. On these trips he learned how to sail in the rough North Atlantic waters.

As a young man, Cartier traveled on a Portuguese trading ship to Brazil. What he really wanted, however, was the chance to explore Newfoundland and discover what lay beyond the coastline. So Cartier talked to King Francis I of France. Cartier promised the king that he would search for gold, spices, and a northwest route to Asia.

Jacques Cartier (1494–1557)

WORDS to KNOW

inscription: a carved message.

interpreter: someone who translates from one language into another.

The king agreed to pay for his ships and supplies. For Cartier, it was the chance of a lifetime.

On April 20, 1534, Cartier sailed from Saint-Malo with two ships and about 120 men. When he landed on Newfoundland, his men put up a 30-foot cross with the **inscription** "Long Live the King of France." The local chief, named Donnacona, objected. He rightly guessed that the French were trying to claim the land.

In response, Cartier kidnapped Donnacona's two sons. Cartier promised Donnacona that he would take good care of them. He wanted to take them to France but he would bring them back, along with many goods. Reluctantly, the old chief agreed.

Cartier then sailed northeast, where he discovered an enormous opening in the coastline that stretched inland as far as he could see.

He thought that he had finally found the fabled Northwest Passage to China. In reality, he was looking at the mouth of the great St. Lawrence River. Cartier wanted to follow the passage west, but he knew that winter was fast approaching. So he headed across the Atlantic for France.

When he arrived home, he told the king that he might have found the Northwest Passage. King Francis was disappointed that Cartier had not brought back any treasures. But he was hopeful that a route to the east would bring riches to France. So he agreed to send Cartier on a second expedition.

DID YOU KNOW?

On his first voyage in 1534, Jacques Cartier saw a strange animal that he described as a large, clumsy ox with two tusks like those of an elephant. It was a walrus.

In May 1535, Cartier set sail again. This time he planned to explore the St. Lawrence River, which he believed would lead him to Asia. He took three ships, about 110 men, and Donnacona's two sons. During their time in France, the young natives had learned to speak French fairly well. This made them useful as guides and **interpreters** to Cartier.

When he reached the New World, Cartier entered the St. Lawrence River. Cartier noticed that the water was salty and had regular tides. It had to lead to the western sea!

As they sailed, the young natives pointed up river and told Cartier that they were nearing the village of Stadacona, where their father ruled. They also told Cartier that farther up, the waterway narrowed and the water turned fresh. Disappointed, Cartier realized that this was probably not his passageway to Asia.

Nevertheless, he and his men continued sailing up the river, exploring the land. A vast wilderness surrounded them. They spotted many animals, including elk, deer, and moose. Salmon, eels, and **lampreys** filled the waters. They even saw creatures such as the beluga whale, which they had never before seen.

WORDS *to* KNOW

lamprey: an eel-like fish.

herbal brew: a kind of tea made with different herbs. These are plants used to add flavor to food or as medicine.

When they reached the village of Stadacona, Chief Donnacona greeted Cartier and was happily reunited with his sons. Because it was too late in the year to sail back to France, Cartier and his crew prepared for winter in Canada. They built a fort, stacked firewood, and salted stores of meat and fish.

The winter months were harsh. Many of the men came down with scurvy. Twenty-five Frenchmen died, and those remaining were ill. During a visit with the chief's son, Cartier learned how to make an **herbal brew** that cured scurvy. Within a week after drinking the medicine, the men grew strong again.

As spring returned, Cartier knew that it was time to sail home. He still had not found the Northwest Passage. Nor had he found any gold or treasure to bring back to King Francis.

Donnacona the Indian chief had talked about a rich kingdom to the north, called Saguenay.

Cartier wanted to tell the king about this wealthy kingdom, but he worried that the king wouldn't believe him. So he decided to kidnap Donnacona. He would have the chief personally tell the king about the treasures of Saguenay. Cartier promised the natives that he would return their chief to them within a year.

Unfortunately, Donnacona died from European diseases before he ever met the king. But the king wanted Cartier to establish a French colony in the New World anyway, to challenge Spain's claims to North America. Cartier had a hard time recruiting volunteers to settle in North America's cold wilderness. He was forced to accept criminals from prisons.

In May 1541, Cartier left on his third voyage to North America. It was his largest voyage yet, with five ships and about 1,500 men. Cartier landed in Canada and made his way to Stadacona. When the natives came to meet him, they asked about their chief. Carter told them that the old chief had died.

Worried that the natives would attack, Cartier sailed his ships farther upstream. He established the first French colony in North America and named it Charlesbourg-Royal. Cartier was also thrilled to discover **nuggets** that looked like gold, and crystals that looked like diamonds.

WORDS *to* KNOW

nugget: a small lump or chunk of something.

iron pyrite: a common mineral that has a pale yellow color.

transparent: clear or see-through.

He was certain that he had finally found New World treasure.

But the French colonists at Charlesbourg-Royal grew uneasy. The neighboring natives no longer trusted them and the French feared they would be massacred. After a long, harsh winter, the colonists were eager to leave. They loaded their ships and sailed for France. They still had not found the Northwest Passage, but Cartier hoped the king would be pleased with the gold and diamonds he found.

In France, a devastated Cartier learned that his New World treasures were worthless. His gold was **iron pyrite** or fool's gold. His diamonds were only a **transparent** mineral, worth nothing. His expedition was considered a failure. There was no colony and no treasure. Cartier spent the rest of his life in Saint-Malo and died there in 1557 at the age of 66.

Despite his failures, Cartier was the first to claim what is now Canada for the French. He also discovered the great Saint Lawrence River, which would later become more valuable than a gold mine. And his reports gave Europeans a great deal of knowledge about the New World. Nevertheless, France would not show interest again in North America for more than half a century.

Martin Frobisher

In June 1576, British explorer Martin Frobisher set out from England in search of the Northwest Passage that would lead to the Indies. His three small ships struggled in the treacherous North Atlantic Ocean. One sank and another was swamped in a storm. Frobisher sailed ahead into the islands and inlets of northeastern North America. He sailed through the bay on Baffin Island that is now named after him. Frobisher mistakenly believed that this bay led to the fabled Northwest Passage. He was excited by soil samples that he believed held gold. With his discoveries, Frobisher sailed back to England.

England was hungry for the gold that Spain had been looting from Central America. When Queen Elizabeth I heard that Frobisher may have found gold, she gave him money for two more voyages. Frobisher sailed again in 1577 and 1578. Both voyages were failures. On these trips, he failed to bring back any gold. He was also unsuccessful at starting a settlement.

After his third voyage, the Queen pulled her support and Frobisher fell into disfavor. Although he never returned to the New World, he regained favor by fighting for the English against the Spanish Armada. During a fight with Spanish forces in 1595, Frobisher was wounded and died. ∿

Settlement at Jamestown

In May 1607, three ships carrying more than 100 English settlers sailed up the James River in present-day Virginia and landed near the Chesapeake Bay. They established a settlement called Jamestown, in honor of King James I.

Jamestown was the first English settlement in America. From the start, the settlers faced many hardships—intense heat, swarms of insects, unsafe water, fierce winters, starvation, disease, and native attacks. The settlers themselves added to the problems. Many were adventurers who wanted to look for gold, not work to develop a colony.

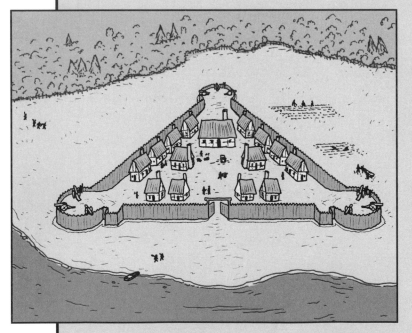

In 1608, Captain John Smith took control of the settlement. He forced the settlers to stop looking for gold and start working to help the colony survive. Injury forced John Smith to return to England in 1609. Without his leadership, the colony floundered. Many died of disease and starvation.

The settlers were about to abandon Jamestown when new colonists and supplies arrived. With the reinforcements, the English decided to push farther into the surrounding area. Each man received his own plot of land to farm. Determined to succeed, the new colonists worked hard to make their individual plots and the community prosperous. By 1685, there were about 70,000 colonists in Virginia. Although Jamestown would be destroyed in a fire in the late 1600s, Virginia would become the birthplace for many of America's early leaders. ∾

Henry Hudson

Henry Hudson was born in England around the time of Jacques Cartier's death. Like Cabot and Cartier, Hudson was convinced that a Northwest Passage to Asia existed. And he wanted to try a new way of getting there. He planned to sail due north—straight across the North Pole—to reach the other side of the world. Hudson thought that if he sailed during the warmer summer months, he just might make it.

Henry Hudson (1565–1611)

Hudson convinced the British Muscovy Company to sponsor his voyage. In 1607, he boarded a small ship named the *Hopewell* with a crew of 12 men. His son, John Hudson, also joined him. In the beginning, the weather was good. But as they neared Greenland, freezing winds and thick fog slowed the ship's progress. Although they came closer to the North Pole than any other explorer, they were still unable to find a way through. With supplies running low, Hudson decided to return to England.

In April 1608, Hudson sailed again on the *Hopewell*. This time he would try to sail east around the North Pole. As they rounded the northern tip of Norway, Hudson and his crew made an amazing discovery.

DID YOU KNOW?

Henry Hudson's crew claimed they saw a strange and beautiful creature in the cold Arctic waters. It had the tail of a porpoise and the body of a woman—a mermaid!

In the Arctic summer, the sun shone for 24 hours a day!

Even with all the sun, however, the wind and waters were still freezing. More and more ice surrounded the ship the farther north they sailed. Eventually the crew grew tired of the cold. Hudson wanted to continue searching, but he agreed to head home for England.

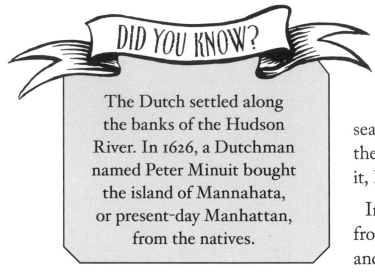

DID YOU KNOW?

The Dutch settled along the banks of the Hudson River. In 1626, a Dutchman named Peter Minuit bought the island of Mannahata, or present-day Manhattan, from the natives.

As news of his voyages traveled across Europe, the Dutch East India Company in Amsterdam agreed to sponsor Hudson's third voyage. They told him to search for a passage to the east of the North Pole. If he could not find it, he was to sail home.

In April 1609, Hudson sailed from Amsterdam on the *Half Moon* and headed north. Once again, ice blocked his way. As the weather grew cold and stormy, the crew began to talk of mutiny. Hudson decided to disobey his orders to return home if he couldn't find a passage. Instead he sailed west towards the New World.

He eventually landed near present-day Maine. Heading south along the coastline, he found the mouth of a great river—the present-day Hudson River. Excited, he thought he may have found the route to the East!

Hudson sailed up the river, exploring the surrounding land.

He sailed about 150 miles to present-day Albany, New York. Here the river became narrow and shallow. Hudson realized that this river was not the passage to the East. But he claimed the Hudson River Valley for Holland. The Dutch would settle this land and call it New Amsterdam. Eventually it would become present-day New York.

Disappointed, Hudson returned home, but in April 1610 he set sail again. On this fourth voyage, Hudson sailed through an icy passage in northern Canada that is called the Hudson Strait today. The strait opened into a great body of water that Hudson believed was the sea route to the Pacific Ocean. In fact, the large body of water was a bay that would become known as Hudson Bay.

As Hudson explored the bay, it became very icy. By November, the ship was frozen in for the winter. Over the long, cold months, food was in short supply and the men grew cold, hungry, and sick. When the ice finally melted in the spring, they wanted to return to England. When Hudson refused, the crew mutinied. They forced Hudson, his son, and several other sick men into a rowboat. The sailors set Hudson adrift in the icy waters of Hudson Bay without food or water.

Hudson and the men in the rowboat were never seen again. It is assumed that they either froze or starved to death.

Although Hudson never found the Northwest Passage, his expeditions increased European knowledge of the world. Today, many places are named after him, from the Hudson Strait and Hudson Bay in Canada, to the Hudson River and the Henry Hudson Parkway in New York.

WORDS *to* KNOW

fur trade: one of the earliest and most important industries in North America. Natives gave furs to Europeans in exchange for tools and weapons.

trading post: a place in the wilderness where people trade things.

Samuel de Champlain (1565–1635)

Samuel de Champlain

In the early 1600s, a French explorer named Samuel de Champlain continued Jacques Cartier's exploration of North America. His mission was to find a good site to start a French settlement. The French were interested in the valuable **fur trade**.

When he arrived, Champlain mapped the land and established fur **trading posts**. In 1604, he began exploring areas south of the St. Lawrence River, including present-day Nova Scotia. He also explored and mapped much of New England, as far south as the Massachusetts Bay.

In 1608, Champlain and about 30 colonists founded a French settlement that would become the city of Quebec. Only nine colonists survived the first winter. A new group of settlers arrived in the spring and the colony began to flourish. Champlain formed alliances with local native groups that would help protect future fur trading settlements.

The French territory in the New World became known as New France. In 1612, the king made Champlain governor of New France. Under Champlain's guidance, the French were able to settle in the area permanently. Although Champlain died from illness in 1635, his influence still exists in North America.

DID YOU KNOW?

The Dutch and the English fought three wars over the land Hudson discovered. In 1664, the English gained control of New Amsterdam and changed its name to New York.

Beginning with the Portuguese in the 1400s and lasting into early 1700s, the Age of Discovery was an exciting time for Europe.

With each journey and discovery, Europeans learned a little bit more about the world. They established direct contact with other cultures in Africa, Asia, and the Americas. People who had never met before shared plants, animals, food, and cultures across continents.

The brave explorers of the New World risked their lives and fortunes with each voyage into the unknown. Their journeys to the New World left a lasting legacy. It can still be seen in the languages, religions, and cultures of the people who live in North and South America today.

MAKE YOUR OWN
CORN BREAD

Native Americans made corn bread from ground corn, salt, and water. Corn was very easy to grow in most parts of North America. It was a staple ingredient in many native dishes.

1 Preheat oven to 425 degrees Fahrenheit (220 degrees Celsius).

2 Combine all ingredients in a mixing bowl and stir well to form a batter. Pour the batter into the greased baking pan.

3 Bake in the oven for about 20 to 25 minutes, until the corn bread turns golden brown.

4 Enjoy it plain or with butter and jam!

SUPPLIES

- Y oven
- Y mixing bowl
- Y measuring cups and spoons
- Y 1 cup cornmeal
- Y 1 cup flour
- Y 2 tablespoons sugar
- Y 4 teaspoons baking powder
- Y $\frac{1}{2}$ teaspoon salt
- Y 1 cup milk
- Y $\frac{1}{4}$ cup vegetable oil
- Y 1 egg beaten
- Y baking pan, 8 or 9 inches square (20 or 23 centimeters)
- Y pot holders
- Y butter and jam

MAKE YOUR OWN
DREAM CATCHER

According to Native American beliefs, dream catchers trap bad dreams and let only good dreams filter down to the sleeper.

1 Bend your twig into a hoop and wrap a short piece of thin wire around the overlapping ends.

2 Cut a few feet of twine or string (about 90 centimeters). Tie one end to the twig hoop. String a few beads on the twine and wrap it around the opposite side of the hoop.

3 Repeat the previous step, going back and forth. Your hoop will have a decorative webbed design.

4 String a few pieces of twine from the bottom of the hoop. Add beads and feathers to hang down from the hoop. Hang the dream catcher near your bed!

SUPPLIES

- bendable twig about 1 foot long (30 centimeters)
- a few inches of thin wire ($7\frac{1}{2}$ centimeters)
- scissors
- twine or string
- beads with large holes
- feathers

MAKE YOUR OWN FELT BEAVER HAT

French explorers traded for fur with Native Americans. This fur trade created a craze in Europe for fur hats!

1 Cut out the center of your paper plate so just the rim is left. Make sure that the rim fits well around your head. Paint the entire plate rim black or brown and set it aside to dry.

2 Cut a piece of cardboard about 6 inches by 25 inches (15 by $63\frac{1}{2}$ centimeters). You may have to staple two pieces together to make one long strip.

3 Make a cylinder with the cardboard to fit just over your plate rim. Staple the cardboard ends together to secure the cylinder.

4 Cut a circular piece of felt to cover the top of the cylinder. Make the felt piece slightly larger than the cylinder so that about one inch hangs down the sides ($2\frac{1}{2}$ centimeters). Glue or staple the felt to the cylinder.

5 Cover the cylinder's body with felt and secure with tape, glue, or staples.

6 When the plate rim is dry, tape the cylinder's open end to the rim. Try on your new beaver hat!

CLASSROOM CONNECTION:
Set up a trading post with your classmates. Divide half the class into Native Americans and half into Europeans. The Native Americans can trade corn bread or dream catchers to the Europeans for small trinkets such as pencils, pennies, or beads. Who will make the best deal?

SUPPLIES

- ¥ paper plate, approximately 10 inches in diameter ($25\frac{1}{2}$ centimeters)
- ¥ scissors
- ¥ black or brown paint
- ¥ paintbrush
- ¥ flexible cardboard from cereal box or manila file folder
- ¥ stapler
- ¥ several pieces of black or brown felt
- ¥ glue or tape

Glossary

A

Admiral: a high rank in the navy that places a person in charge of a fleet of ships.

Age of Exploration and Discovery: a period in history from the early 1400s to the early 1600s, when Europeans explored and mapped the world.

alliance: a partnership between peoples or countries.

Americas: the land and islands of North, South, and Central America.

anchor: to lower a heavy metal hook to the ocean floor to stop a ship from drifting.

Arabs: a group of people that comes from the Arabian Peninsula.

astrolabe: an instrument used to measure the height of celestial bodies above the horizon.

astronomer: a person who studies the stars, planets, and sky.

astronomy: the study of stars, planets, and space.

Aztecs: Mexican native people who built a great civilization before the conquest of Mexico by Cortés.

B

bacteria: very tiny living things that decay food and can be harmful.

balsa: a very light wood.

bandit: a thief.

barricade: a barrier to stop people from getting past a certain point.

bullying: forcing someone to do what you want or treating a weaker person badly.

C

caravel: a small Portuguese or Spanish sailing ship, usually with triangular sails on two or three masts.

cargo: goods carried by a ship.

cartographer: a person who makes maps.

causeway: a raised road built across water or low ground.

celestial: to do with the sky or the heavens.

ceremony: an event to celebrate or honor something, such as a god or a holiday.

channel: a narrow stretch of water between two areas of land.

circumnavigate: to go all the way around.

colonist: someone who settles a new area.

colonize: to settle in another country.

Glossary

compass: a device that uses a magnet to show which direction is north.

conquistadors: Spanish conquerors of the Americas in the 1500s.

convert: to change a person's religious beliefs.

cove: a small, sheltered inlet along a coast.

criminal: a person who has committed a crime.

crossbow: a weapon used to shoot arrows.

current: the movement of water in a river or an ocean.

D

devout: deeply religious.

dysentery: an infection of the intestines.

E

equator: an imaginary line around the earth, halfway between the North and South Poles.

evade: to keep away or avoid.

expedition: a long voyage with a goal.

F

Far East: area including East and Southeast Asia.

fleet: a group of ships traveling together.

foliage: the leaves of plants and trees.

fur trade: one of the earliest and most important industries in North America. Natives gave furs to Europeans in exchange for tools and weapons.

G

galley: a long ship with oars, used for war or trading. Also a ship's kitchen.

geographer: a person who studies the earth's surface and its people, plants, and animals.

glaciers: huge sheets of ice found in mountains or polar regions.

H

harbor: a place where ships shelter or unload their cargo.

herbal brew: a kind of tea made with different herbs. These are plants used to add flavor to food or as medicine.

horizon: the line in the distance where the land or sea seems to meet the sky.

Glossary

hull: the hollow, lowest part of a ship.

humidity: moisture in the air.

I

ice breaker: a ship that can break a channel through the ice.

immunity: able to resist a disease.

inland: away from the sea.

inlet: a narrow body of water that leads inland from a larger body of water.

inscription: a carved message.

integrate: to become part of.

interpreter: someone who translates from one language into another.

iron pyrite: a common mineral that has a pale yellow color.

L

lamprey: an eel-like fish.

land grant: a gift of land.

lateen: a triangular sail on a ship.

latitude: the position of a place, measured in degrees north or south of the equator.

legendary: famous.

litter: a stretcher used to carry someone.

longitude: lines perpendicular to the equator, measuring distance east or west from a point in England.

loot: to steal money or treasure.

M

mainland: the land of a continent.

maneuver: to move something carefully into position.

mariner: sailor.

maritime: having to do with the sea and sailing.

massacre: brutal killing of a large number of people.

merchant: someone who buys and sells goods for a profit.

monarch: a ruler such as a king or queen.

monopoly: complete control of something, like a service or product.

Moors: people from North Africa.

mutiny: a rebellion of the ship's crew against its captain.

N

native people: people with their own culture who live in an area before anyone arrives from another country.

Glossary

navigation: method of finding your way and figuring out your location.

navigator: a person who works to find or direct a route, usually by sea.

New World: North and South America.

noble: a person of high rank or birth.

Northeast Passage: a sea route along the northern coast of Europe and Asia, connecting the Atlantic and Pacific oceans.

Northern Hemisphere: the half of the earth north of the equator.

North Star: the brightest star in the Northern Hemisphere. It is at the end of the handle of the Little Dipper.

Northwest Passage: a sea route along the northern coast of North America, connecting the Atlantic and Pacific Oceans.

nugget: a small lump or chunk of something.

O

Ottoman Empire: an empire based in Turkey that controlled North Africa, southern Europe, and Southwest Asia.

Ottoman Turks: rulers of the Ottoman Empire.

outpost: a remote settlement.

P

padrão: a large stone pillar carved with Portugal's coat of arms. It was placed by explorers to claim land.

passage: a sea route.

pension: an amount of money paid at regular times for past service.

pike: a long wooden pole with a steel head.

preserve: to dry, smoke, or salt food so it won't spoil.

prosperous: wealthy.

province: a district or region of some countries.

provisions: supplies of food.

putrid: decaying and smelling bad.

Q

quadrant: an instrument to measure the height of the planets, moon, or stars.

quarters: living space.

quest: a search for something.

Glossary

R

rations: the amount of food given for each meal.

reef: a strip of rock or coral close to the surface of the water.

resource: anything to help people take care of themselves, such as water, food, and building materials.

retaliate: to fight back.

revenue: income or money.

revolt: to fight against a government or person of authority.

rigging: the ropes and wires on a ship that support and control the sails.

rival: a person or group that competes with another.

S

scurvy: a disease common among sailors, caused by the lack of vitamin C in the diet. Vitamin C is found in fruits like oranges.

settlement: a place where a group of people moves to start a new community.

siege: surrounding a place, such as a city, to cut off supplies. It forces those inside to eventually surrender.

Silk Road: the ancient network of trade routes connecting the Mediterranean Sea and China by land.

slave: a person owned by another person and forced to work without pay.

smallpox: a deadly disease.

sphere: round, like a ball.

sponsor: to give money and support.

strait: a narrow stretch of water that connects two larger bodies of water.

T

terrain: ground or land.

trading post: a place in the wilderness where people trade things.

trading route: a route used to carry goods from one place to be sold in another.

transparent: clear or see-through.

travelogue: a written account of a journey or travels.

Resources

Books

Aronson, Marc. *The World Made New: Why the Age of Exploration Happened and How It Changed the World.* National Geographic Children's Books, Washington D.C.: 2007.

Bailey, Katharine, *Vasco da Gama: Quest for the Spice Trade.* Crabtree Publishing Company, NY: 2007.

Bergreen, Lawrence. *Over the Edge of the World: Magellan's Terrifying Circumnavigation of the Globe.* Harper Perennial, NY: 2004.

Dor-Ner, Zvi, and William Scheller. *Columbus and the Age of Discovery.* William Morrow and Company, Inc., NY: 1991.

Fritz, Jean. *Around the World in a Hundred Years: From Henry the Navigator to Magellan.* Putnam & Grosset Group. NY: 1994.

Fritze, Ronald. *New Worlds: The Great Voyages of Discovery, 1400–1600.* Praeger, NY: 2003.

Horwitz, Tony. *A Voyage Long and Strange.* Henry Holt and Company, NY: 2008.

Mattox, Jake. *Explorers of the New World.* Greenhaven Press, MN: 2003.

Riggenburgh, Beau. *National Geographic Society Exploration Experience.* National Geographic Society, Washington, D.C.: 2007.

Sansevere-Dreher, Diane. *Explorers Who Got Lost.* Tor Books, NY: 1992.

Zronik, John. *Francisco Pizarro: Journeys through Peru and South America.* Crabtree Publishing Company, NY: 2005.

Web Sites

The Mariners Museum. Visit an online exhibit about the Age of Exploration.
http://marinersmuseum.org

Conquistadors On-line Learning Adventure, PBS.org.
http://www.pbs.org/opb/conquistadors/home.htm

The European Voyages of Exploration.
http://www.ucalgary.ca/applied_history/tutor/eurvoya/index.html

Collection of information and sources about explorers.
http://www.win.tue.nl/cs/fm/engels/discovery/

Discovery: The Beginnings.
http://www.wsu.edu:8080/~dee/reform/begin.htm

National Maritime Museum: Sea and Ships.
http://www.nmm.ac.uk/explore/sea-and-ships/

Links to documents related to the Age of Exploration.
http://www.historyteacher.net/APEuroCourse/WebLinks/WebLinks-AgeOfExploration.html

Index

Index

Index